BEFORE & AFTER SCHOOL PROGRAMS:
A START-UP AND ADMINISTRATION MANUAL

by
Mary McDonald Richard

SCHOOL-AGE NOTES
P.O. Box 40205
Nashville, TN
37204-0205

MARY MCDONALD RICHARD has provided start-up, consultation and coordination services to numerous before and after school programs and school administrators. Additionally, Ms. Richard has held positions as an elementary Art and Spanish teacher and has served as the Administrator/Coordinator of a licensed child care center. She has conducted state and regional workshops about school-age child care topics, and has worked as an organization consultant for child care concerns since 1980.

BEFORE & AFTER SCHOOL PROGRAMS:
A START-UP AND ADMINISTRATION MANUAL

Published by: School-Age NOTES
P.O. Box 40205
Nashville, TN 37204-0205
(615) 242-8464

Book design by BASP Resources

Printed by: BookCrafters
Chelsea, Michigan

ACKNOWLEDGEMENTS

I would like to acknowledge the contributions of many people to *Before and After School Programs: A Start-Up and Administration Manual.*

The parents and staff of the Before and After School Programs in the Iowa City's public schools are acknowledged for the many "real-life" situations, from which arose the impetus to create and compile school-age resources. The Iowa City 4 C's agency is acknowledged for its support of these programs.

Kathy Robinson-Kramer, Day Care Consultant, Iowa Department of Human Services, Craig Welt, CPCU, and my husband, Dell A. Richard, attorney-at-law, provided valuable counsel and support.

Further, I would like to acknowledge the vision and enthusiasm of the early childhood consultants in Iowa's area education agencies and Department of Education, who have encouraged me in this project.

I am especially grateful for the constant inspiration, support, encouragement and patience of my school-agers, John Andrew and Michael Thomas.

Mary McDonald Richard

BEFORE AND AFTER SCHOOL PROGRAMS:
A *START-UP AND ADMINISTRATION MANUAL*

TABLE OF CONTENTS

A START-UP RESOURCES

B BUDGETS AND PAYROLL

C APPLICATION FOR TAX-EXEMPT STATUS

D PARENT HANDBOOK

E BOARD MANUAL

F STAFF RECRUITMENT AND EMPLOYMENT MODEL PROCEDURES AND FORMS

G STAFF HANDBOOK

H A STATEMENT-BASED APPROACH TO STAFF EVALUATION

I FORM BOOK

J SUBSTITUTE CAREGIVER EMPLOYMENT

K PLANNING THE DAILY SCHEDULE

REFERENCES AND RESOURCES

INTRODUCTION

This manual was designed for start-up and administration of parent-run programs in the schools. However, the information, ideas and forms can be applied to or adapted for other school-age child care situations. All legal forms are intended as samples only, for use by attorneys licensed to practice in the jurisdiction where the forms are being used.

A computer software version of this manual to allow easy adaptation and customization of the forms is available. Contact School-Age NOTES for more information.

Local Variables and Considerations

There are many variables that affect start-up and implementation of school-age programs. The following are some of these variables and corresponding considerations:

Full-day, part-day or half-day kindergarten - Affects staffing, programming and space use of the child care program

Non-profit, not-for-profit or for-profit status - Affects fees, budget and parent involvement in the child care program

Type of space, "dedicated space" (space used solely by program) versus shared space, such as the use of school cafeterias, gyms, classrooms or church facilities - Affects implementation of a quality program.

Year-round school versus traditional school calendar - Affects staffing, space, programming and budget of the child care program

Whether both before and after school child care is needed - Affects staffing because of split-shift, part-time work

Background of Example Program

The information and forms in this manual are based on actual experience in starting and administering before and after school programs. However, the scenarios, applications and other forms in the manual use the name of a fictional parent-run program, Washington Before and After School Program which is located in Washington Elementary School, in the River City School District of River City, Iowa.

Washington Before and After School Program (WBASP) operates every school day from 7 AM to 8:30 AM and 3:00 PM to 6:00 PM, utilizing the gym, two kindergarten rooms, kitchen and two bathrooms of Washington Elementary School. At other times these facilities are regularly used by organizations including Scouts, Camp Fire, P.T.A., foreign language and aerobics classes.

WBASP was started by a committee of Washington parents who, in cooperation with the school principal and district administrators, developed and implemented the program. It is self-supporting, deriving its operational support primarily from parent fees of the children who are registered and enrolled. The school provides in-kind donations of space, utilities, furniture, A/V equipment, and school custodial services.

The program's license permits no more than thirty children to be on site at any time. Thirty six full and part-time children are enrolled. Staff-child ratio is approximately 1:10.

Summer Care and Full Day Care

After initially starting a before and after school program that operates only on school days, many programs realize that responding to the needs of children of working parents may mean exploring summer care and full care on the week days when school is not in session. Staffing patterns, budgets, additional fees, programming and provisions for meals must be analyzed in consideration of full-day care.

A

BEFORE & AFTER SCHOOL PROGRAM

START-UP RESOURCES

PROJECT START-UP

The following steps are listed in the order that actions should be taken to start a Before and After School program. Individual projects may vary somewhat from the order, however no step may be skipped. Supplementary materials found in this manual are indicated with *.

1.   Identify people who are willing to form an start-up committee for the project. Some of these will need to serve as start-up chairperson, treasurer, secretary, and professional advisors.

2.*   Obtain copies of your state's child care license application form and a copy of the regulations booklet of child care licensing standards from your local office of the state child care licensing agency.

3.   Study the licensing standards and regulations booklet; note regulations which govern the operation of school-age child care centers.

4.   The start-up committee or a designated representative should meet with the building principal to express interest in the implementation of a before and after school child care program. Issues to be discussed include: physical location of the program in building facilities (classrooms, gym, kitchen, media center, special rooms, playground, storage space), as well as what school equipment might be used (A.V., sports equipment, etc.).

5.   Schedule an appointment with the day care consultant from your licensing agency at the school. He or she will be able to consult with representatives from the school and start-up committee regarding the facilities being considered for license, as well as other required and/or recommended procedures for child care center start-up.

6.   A representative from the start-up committee should give an informational presentation to the school P.T.A. The committee may to consider whether it would be appropriate to request financial support or a "no-interest" start-up loan.

7.*   Print and distribute through the school a **Child Care Needs Survey**. Evaluate responses.

8.*   Contact carriers of liability and workers compensation insurance. Obtain proposals and select amount and cost of coverage.

9.*   Draw up a start-up and operating budget for the program. Determine the expenses as related to the number of children which you wish to accomodate during the first year. Combinations of part and full time enrollments may be figured as "FTE" (full-time equivalent) enrollments. Factors which will determine program size, as well as tuition include: size of facility to be licensed, number of enrollments, amount of fee and tuition income, number of staff to be employed, and start-up and operating expenses.

10.*   Apply for Federal I.D. number ("42" number) by calling the IRS (1-816-996-5999), and request tax forms (1-800-424-3676).

11.   Open a bank account.

12.   Consult with bookkeeper or accountant. Determine bookkeeping system and procedures/forms to be used for handling money.

13.*   Determine program policies and procedures for parents. Prepare Parent handbook, including tuition schedule and directory of the Board of Directors.

14.   Hold a school informational/registration meeting. Have registration forms as well as program policies available for prospective program parents.

15.   Consult with legal advisors and file for non-profit incorporation.

16.*   Draw up By-Laws. An attorney may do this along with the incorporation papers.

17.*   Start to compile Board Manuals for each member of the Board of Directors.

18.   Contact the local Fire Marshall regarding a required inspection.

19.   Contact the County Health Department regarding a required inspection.

20.*   Adapt Child and Staff forms for use in your school program. You may need only to embellish those provided with your program name and logo. If used other than in the state of Iowa, you should clear these forms for use with your local office of the state child care licensing agency.

21.*   Set up record keeping system for staff and children. Secure a supply of Employer Verification forms and Internal Revenue Service forms.

22.*   Confirm, print and distribute space/equipment usage agreement with school.

23.*   Determine job descriptions, policies and procedures for staff. Prepare Staff Handbook. Prepare staff contracts in accordance with the contents of the handbook.

24.*   Recruit and employ the Child Care Director.

25.*   Board and Child Care Director work together to develop program; design curriculum, daily schedules for staff and children, plan weekly planning procedures and record forms.

26.*   Prepare program bulletin board of postings required by the licensing regulations.

27.   Prepare postings of fire and tornado procedures for exits.

28.*   Child Care Director and Board hire aides.

29.*   Develop snack program and schedule first month's food.

30.*   Schedule first month's activities.

31.   Send notes to parents regarding donations of games, supplies and refrigerator.

32.   Contact food and supply vendors regarding discounts.

33.   Contact businesses regarding free resources.

34.   Ask for volunteers to serve as guest speakers, mentors, etc.

35.*   Apply for tax-exempt status within the first fifteen months.

SURVEY ON BEFORE & AFTER SCHOOL CHILD CARE

An organizing committee has been formed to study implementation of a before and after child care program at _____ beginning in the fall, 1992. The program which would be located at the school and would care for children grades K-6 before and after school.

If sufficient interest is present, as indicated by the results of this survey, a board of directors will be formed, a Child Care Director hired, and a budget and activity program developed. The program will be licensed by the Department of Human Services, and for the purpose of obtaining tax-exempt status from the Internal Revenue Service, the program would be incorporated in the state of Iowa as a non-profit corporation.

The objective of this survey is to assess before and after school child care needs of families whose children attend our school. **Your response is not a commitment to enrolling your child in the program; it is solely for the purpose of providing the organizing committee with information.**

For more information, please feel free to contact:

Complete lower portion of this form and return to the school.

*   *   *   *   *   *   *   *   *   *   *   *

CHILD CARE SURVEY RESPONSE

PLEASE RETURN TO SCHOOL BY _____

Would you be interested in enrolling your child(ren) in a before and after school child care program at _____ in the fall of 1992?

_____Yes, before school only from _____AM (to start of school)
_____Yes, after school only until _____PM
_____Yes, both before and after school from _____AM to _____PM
_____Yes, before school and conference days
_____Yes, after school and conference days
_____Yes, before and after school and conference days
_____No

Number of Children and Ages you may be interested in enrolling:

Number_____   Age(s)_____

Are you interested in assisting with the development of a before and after school program? If yes, please indicate your name and phone number:

Name_____Phone#_____

SPACE/EQUIPMENT AGREEMENT

The following sample agreement represents a composite of ideas and information useful to before and after school programs staff and boards, school principals, staff and teachers who utilize school building space and facilities. The BASP Board of Directors will want to modify it to suit the particular needs of the school and the program.

The Before and After School Program of _____ School ("Program") and _____ Elementary School ("School") have agreed to the following arrangements as provided hereafter:

HOURS:
The premises shall be used for a weekday program of not more than 30 children from 7:00 am to 8:30 am and from 3:00 pm (Th) to 6:00 pm.

PRIMARY LOCATION OF THE PROGRAM:
Rooms 100, 101, and two bathrooms, located in the hallway area in front of these rooms will be the primary location of the Program.

CLASSROOM SPACE AND STORAGE:
The Program will have full use of all chairs and tables in the classrooms.

The Program will have full use of the sink, drinking fountain and counter space in room 101.

Program files and supplies may be kept in the lower right cabinet of the built-in storage on the south wall of Room 101.

Coats and personal belongings of children in the program may be located in the open locker spaces in Room 100 during program hours. The lockers must be vacated after the program ends each morning and afternoon.

The School reserves the built-in counter space on the south wall of each room for school projects which are to be undisturbed by the program.

The teacher desks and personal coat areas are not to be used by the Program. Any writing on the chalkboards which is marked "Save" must be preserved.

The Program will supply all of its own scissors, pencils, markers, and various other classroom supplies. The Program may not use school supplies frequently found in the classroom.

GYM AND STORAGE:

The gym may be used by the Program on a daily basis.

The program may use only permanent fixtures of the gym designated by the gym teacher. This shall exclude use of the climbing rope and climbing net. Mats may be used by permission. The Program will provide its own consumable equipment such as basketballs.

The Program may place a large storage cabinet in the gym for storage of program supplies. The School reserves the right to approve the appearance of the cabinet before it becomes a permanent item.

In the event that the gym is to be set up with chairs for a meeting, the School will notify the Program three days in advance.

KITCHEN, REFRIGERATOR AND STORAGE:

The Program may use the kitchen for preparing snacks and two shelves in the cupboard which may be used on a daily basis by the program.

The Program is permitted to place a refrigerator in the kitchen which will be used solely by the Program. The School may approve the refrigerator for size and appearance before it becomes a permanent item.

The School will have priority use of the kitchen for events such as the annual chili supper. If the kitchen is to be used for such an event, the School will notify the Program at least three days in advance.

The Program will supply its own paper supplies and cookware, kitchen utensils and cleaning products.

PLAYGROUND:

The rear portion of the playground, on the west side of the building will be available on a daily basis as a playground. The west door only will be used as access to the playground.

TELEPHONE:

The Program may place a telephone jack in Room 101 at its own expense. The Program may plug in its own phone during program hours for its use.

The Program will pay the School monthly for the difference in the phone bill to provide for the extension phone, and any long distance calls incurred by the Program. School staff will not use the Program telephone.

A.V. EQUIPMENT:

The Program may have access to the use of Media Center A.V. equipment. The educational director should reserve the use of the equipment with the Media Secretary.

All A.V. equipment must be entirely supervised by Program staff; no child in the program shall be permitted to operate equipment or to push carts carrying any A.V. equipment.

ENTRANCE:

The entrance to be used by parents bringing and retrieving their children from the Program will be the East side door of the building.

PARKING:

Parents who come to the school to retrieve children at the end of the day are to park in the marked spaces; not in the fire lane.

AFTER HOURS USE OF THE SCHOOL BUILDING:

The Program may schedule evening meetings Monday through Friday, by reserving space with the school secretary at least a week in advance of the date.

PROGRAM RESPONSIBILITIES:

The Program will lock windows of all program area rooms before leaving each day.

The Program will stack all chairs in Rooms 100 and 101, as well as any taken out for use in the gym, at the end of the day.

The Program will return all chairs and tables to the locations shown on the room arrangement chart which will be provided to them by the School.

The Program agrees to mark all property owned by them which remains on the premises.

The Program will be responsible for assisting maintenance of the program area by daily cleaning of all table tops and by cleaning up any craft or food remains. The Program will leave the premises in as good shape and condition as when entered, normal wear excepted.

The Program will be responsible for any and all breakage of chairs, tables, and play equipment beyond normal wear and tear. The Program shall notify the School office immediately upon discovering any such damage.

The Program will inform its staff about the contents of this agreement and expect their support and compliance.

SCHOOL RESPONSIBILITIES:

The School will daily clear the floor space of papers or non-furniture items which might be disturbed by children in the course of normal activity during the program.

The School will furnish janitorial service to the program by daily vacuuming of the classrooms, cleaning of the bathrooms, trash removal and chalkboard cleaning after the program closing hour of 5:30 pm.

The School will be responsible for structural repairs to building and plumbing therein unless it is determined that the damage has been caused by the act of or negligence of the Program, in which event the Program shall be responsible.

The School will furnish the program with a room arrangement chart of classroom tables and chairs in order that they may be returned to the correct location at the end of each program session.

The School will inform its staff about this agreement and its contents and expect their support and compliance.

FORMAL COMMUNICATION:

In order to prevent friction from occurring, in the event that any need for change occurs or conflict arises regarding the use of space or equipment, the School will communicate through the building principal or his/her designee.

The Program will communicate through the Child Care Director and/or the president of the BASP Board of Directors. It is not expected that Program aides, School custodians or teachers will have ongoing dialogue regarding items covered in this agreement.

RECIPROCAL WAIVER OF SUBROGATION:

The Before and After School Program and the School District each release the other party (which term as used in this paragraph includes employees, agents, officers and directors of the other party) from all liability, whether for negligence or otherwise, in connection with loss covered by any insurance policies which the releasor carries with respect to school property, but only to the extent that such loss is collected under said insurance policies.

Such waiver of subrogation is also conditioned upon the inclusion in the policy or policies of a provision whereby any such waiver shall not adversely affect said policies or prejudice any right of the releasor to recover thereunder. Each party agrees that its insurance policies will include such a provision.

RENEWAL AND MODIFICATION:

This Space Agreement shall continue during the 19____ - 19____ school year, and shall be automatically renewed for each succeeding school year thereafter until terminated by either party upon sixty days written notice. Modifications shall be evidenced in writing and signed by the parties hereto.

I have read this agreement and agree to abide by it to the best of my ability.

_____

Signature of Designated School District Administrator   **Date**

_____

Signature of Building Principal   **Date**

_____

Signature of President of the BASP Board of Directors   **Date**

BY-LAWS

of

THE WASHINGTON ELEMENTARY
BEFORE AND AFTER SCHOOL PROGRAM

ARTICLE I.
Name

The organization shall be called The Washington Elementary Before and After School Program, and shall be a non-profit organization sponsored by interested groups approved by the membership.

ARTICLE II.
Purpose

The Washington Elementary Before and After School Program is a non-profit corporation organized to provide quality before and after school care for children in kindergarten through sixth grades. The purpose of the program is to provide a safe and stimulating environment which is child-centered.

ARTICLE III.
Membership

Section 1.

Members shall include parents or guardians of children enrolled the Before and After School Program, other parents involved with assisting the program, staff members employed by the Program, and the principal of the Washington Elementary School.

Section 2.

Each family shall have a single vote in all elections and decision-making and shall be expected to attend an annual meeting.

Section 3.

Enrollment of children is subject to prompt payment of fees, availability of space, and adherence to program guidelines and rules.

Section 4.

The Washington Elementary Before and After School Program shall not consciously discriminate against anyone because of race, sex, handicap, color, creed, national origin, or ethnic background.

Section 5.

Honorary members may be appointed by the Board, shall have the right to attend and speak at parent meetings, but may not make motions or vote.

ARTICLE IV.
Officers and Elections

Section 1.

Officers shall be the Director, Chairperson(s), Secretary and Treasurer. Duties of the offices are those associated with their position and such other duties as may be determined by the Board of Directors.

Section 2.

Officers shall be elected by the annual general meeting by majority selection from among the members. Officers shall assume their positions immediately upon election.

ARTICLE V.
Board of Directors

Section 1.

The Board of Directors shall be responsible for establishing and maintaining all policies and procedures regarding the operation of this organization including policies regarding the amounts and time of payment of fees. The Board may, however, at its discretion delegate such portions of its authority to the Director as is necessary for the Director to perform his/her duties.

Section 2.

The Board shall consist of Chairperson(s), Secretary, Treasurer, the School Principal, and up to 4 additional voting members. The Director of the Program shall be an ex-officio member of the board, and shall have the right to vote on all matters other than those involving staff employment and evaluation.

Section 3.

The Board shall meet at least quarterly. A quorum of the Board shall consist of at least three members in attendance at a meeting. Meetings of the Board shall be open to all members. The Board reserves the right to enter executive session in the event of confidential matters.

ARTICLE VI.
Staff Personnel

Section 1.

The Director shall be appointed by the Board of Directors which shall establish conditions of salary and employment.

Section 2.

The Director shall hold office at the pleasure of the Board and shall be responsible for the operation of the program under the direction of the Board. Responsibilities of the Director shall include recommendations to the Board on employment, supervision and discharge of other staff positions as may be created by the Board, supervision of other staff members, program design and development, and communication with members on a regular basis.

ARTICLE VII.
General Members Meeting

Section 1.

A meeting open to all members shall be held at least once per year. Additional meetings may be called by the Board acting alone or upon petition by at least 20% of the members.

Section 2.

A quorum at a member meeting shall consist of at least 50% of the membership at the time of the meeting.

Section 3.

Election and Removal of officers shall rest solely within the membership. Election of officers shall occur at the general membership meeting. Removal of Chairperson, Secretary or Treasurer may be accomplished at any general membership meeting but shall require a simple majority of the members present at a meeting where a quorum exists.

ARTICLE VIII.
Amendment of By-Laws

Amendments of by-laws may be recommended by the Board for vote of the members present, subject to consideration and vote of the general membership at the annual meeting.

ARTICLE IX.
Parliamentary Authority

Robert's Rules of Order Revised shall govern all meetings of the Board and general membership in all cases to which they are applicable and in which they are not in conflict with these by-laws.

I hereby certify that the above By-Laws were adopted by the members and Board of Directors of said corporation under resolution at their meeting on the _____ day of _____, 1992.

_____
Secretary

ARTICLES OF INCORPORATION

of

The Washington Elementary Before and After School Program

To The Secretary of State of the State of Iowa:

We, the undersigned, under the Iowa Nonprofit Corporation Act under Chapter 504A, of the 1989 Code of Iowa, as amended, do hereby adopt the following Articles of Incorporation for such corporation:

I.   The name of the corporation shall be known as The Washington Elementary Before and After School Program.

II.   The period of its duration is perpetual.

III.   This corporation is organized and shall operate for the purpose of providing quality before and after school child care for children in kindergarten through sixth grade enrolled the Before and After School Program of Washington Elementary School, River City, Ia. Activities provided shall include educational and recreational activities which contribute to the development of the children. The educational purpose of this organization is limited to those permitted under Section 501(c)(3) of the Internal Revenue Code or its successor sections in subsequent revenue codes.

IV.   The address of its initial registered office in the state of Iowa is 2000 Lakeside Drive in the city of River City, county of Johnson, and the name of its initial registered agent at such address is Kathleen Berg.

V.   The business of this corporation shall be conducted by a Board of Director consisting initially of eight directors, although the number of directors may be increased from time to time as permitted by the By-Laws of this corporation. The initial Directors shall be:

Kathleen Berg	2345 Gleason Ave.	River City, IA 52240
Danielle Holden	3728 Gleason Ave.	River City, IA 52240
Ann Hill	1803 Gleason Ave.	River City, IA 52240
Donna Walker	4507 Crosby Lane	River City, IA 52240
Alan Kindhart	3467 Gleason Drive	River City, IA 52240
Mary Stewart	5677 Burns Ave.	River City, IA 52240
Stephanie Allen	7897 Hollywood Ct.	River City, IA 52240

VI.   The incorporator of this corporation is as follows:

        Kathleen Berg
        2345 Gleason Ave.
        River City, IA 52240

VII.   Members of this corporation shall include parents or guardians of children enrolled in the Washington Elementary Before and After School Program, other parents involved with assisting the program, staff members employed by the program, and the Principal of the Washington Elementary School. There shall be only one class of member of this corporation and there shall be no membership dues required. There is no designation or election process for members of this corporation.

VIII.   The private property of the members of this corporation shall be exempt from corporate debts.

IX.   This corporation shall issue no stock nor shall any dividends be paid to any of the members of this corporation.

X.   This corporation shall have no seal.

XI.   Upon the dissolution of the corporation, the Board of Directors shall, after paying or making provision for the payment of all of the liabilities of the corporation, dispose of all of the assets of the corporation exclusively for the purposes of the corporation in such manner, or to such organization or organizations organized and operated exclusively for charitable, educational, religious, or scientific purposes as shall at the time qualify as an exempt organization or organizations under Section 501(c)(3) of the Internal Revenue Code of 1986 (or the corresponding provision of any future United States Internal Revenue Law), as the Board of Directors shall determine. Any of such assets not so disposed of shall be disposed of by the Johnson County District Court, exclusively for such purposes or to such organization or organizations, as said Court shall determine, which are organized and operated exclusively for such purposes.

XII.   No part of the net earnings of this corporation shall inure to the benefit of, or be distributable to, its members, trustees, officers or other private persons, except that the corporation shall be authorized and empowered to pay reasonable compensation for services rendered and to make payments and distributions in furtherance of the purposes set forth in Article III. hereof. No substantial part of the activities of the corporation shall be the carrying on of propaganda, or otherwise attempting, to influence legislation, and the corporation shall not participate in, or intervene in (including the publishing or distribution of statements) any political campaign on behalf of any candidate for public office. Notwithstanding any other provision of these Articles, the corporation shall not carry on any other activities not permitted to be carried on (a) by a corporation exempt from Federal income tax under Section 501(c)(3) of the Internal Revenue Code of 1986 (or the corresponding provision of any future United States Internal Revenue Law), or (b) by a corporation, contributions to which are deductible under Section 170(c)(2) of the Internal Revenue Code of 1986 (or the corresponding provisions of any future United States Internal Revenue Law).

XIII. No contract or other transaction between the corporation or any other corporation shall be affected or invalidated by the fact that any one or more of the directors of this corporation is or are interested, or is a director or officer, or are directors of officers, of such other corporation, and any director or directors, individually or jointly, may be a party or parties to, or may be interested in, any contract or transaction of this corporation, or in which this corporation is interested; and no contract, act or transaction of this corporation with any person or persons, firm or association shall be affected or invalidated by the fact that any director or directors of this corporation is a party or are parties to or interested in such contract, act or transaction, or in any way connected with such person or persons, firm or association, and each and every person who may become a director of this corporation is hereby relieved of any liability that might otherwise exist from contracting with the corporation for the benefit of himself or any firm or corporation which he may be in any way interested.

XIV. This corporation shall indemnify any present or former director, officer, employee, member or volunteer of this corporation, and each such person who is serving or who has served, at the request of this corporation as a director, officer, partner, trustee, employee or agent of another corporation, partnership, joint venture, trust, other enterprise or employee benefit plan to the fullest extent possible against expenses, including attorneys' fees, judgments, fines, settlements and reasonable expenses, actually incurred by such person relating to his conduct as a director, officer, employee, member or volunteer of this corporation or as a director, officer, partner, trustee, employee or agent of another corporation, partnership, joint venture, trust, other enterprise or employee benefit plan, except that the mandatory indemnification required by this sentence shall not apply (i) to a breach of the duty of loyalty to the corporation, (ii) for acts or omissions not in good faith or which involve intentional misconduct or knowing violation of the law, or (iii) for a transaction from which such person derived an improper personal benefit.

_____
Kathleen Berg

STATE OF IOWA   )
COUNTY OF   ) ss:
JOHNSON   )

     On this ____ day of April, 1992, before, the undersigned, a Notary Public in and for the State of Iowa, personally appeared Kathleen Berg, to me known to be the identical person named in and who executed this instrument, and acknowledged the execution of the same to be her voluntary act and deed.

_____
Notary public in and for the State of Iowa

LICENSING INFORMATION

The following information is specific to the state of Iowa and is shown here as an example of the licensing procedure. Contact your local office of the state child care licensing agency for information on procedures in your state.

APPLICATION FOR A CHILD CARE CENTER LICENSE:

1. At least four months prior to opening the child care program, contact the day care consultant at your county or area office of the state Department of Human Services (DHS) to obtain a child care license application form and other information related to licensing.

2. The application for a license must be filled out and submitted to the DHS by the chairman of the program board of directors which is the program's legal entity.

3. Prior to opening, the Child Care Director and Board of Directors (or a representative(s) of the Board should conduct a license self-study. The DHS Child Care Center Evaluation and Recommendation for License form and the Child Day Care Centers and Preschools Licensing Standards and Procedures booklet are the appropriate tools for use.

    Program board and staff have the responsibility to study the plans, procedures and forms which will be implemented in their program, corresponding to the regulations set out by law. The Child Care Center Evaluation and Recommendation for License form may be used as a self-study checklist. All program aspects must be in conformance with the requirements of this list, as they apply to school-age child care.

4. Three months prior to opening, contact the local Fire Marshall and schedule an inspection of the facilities to be used by the program. This inspection must occur prior the day of opening. The Fire Marshall will issue a Certificate of Inspection Report which he/she will forward to the DHS.

5. A drawing of the floor plan of the facilities used by the program must be made, including all measurements, and a copy forwarded to the DHS. Keep the original to make emergency procedure maps, room charts, etc.

6. Contact the county health department regarding the need to schedule an inspection with the Program shortly after opening. Among their duties, health inspectors may check immunization cards, the food preparation area, snack schedule, etc. There may be a charge for this inspection. The inspector will forward the report to the DHS.

POSTINGS REQUIRED FOR LICENSED CENTERS:

It is suggested that a bulletin board be prepared with the following items and daily displayed in a conspicuous place:

1. The current license.

2. Requirements and procedures for mandatory reporting of suspected child abuse and neglect.

3. A notice stating that a copy of the Child Day Care Centers and Preschools Licensing Standards and Procedures is available upon request from the Child Care Director. The name, office mailing address and telephone number of the DHS day care consultant, should be on the notice.

4. Current month's snack schedule.

5. Copies of emergency plans (drawings and directions) for fire and tornados by all exits. Place the drawing where it "makes sense" when you look at it so that directions may be understood and carried out quickly since substitute personnel or others unfamiliar with the facilities may also be caught in an emergency. A red "You Are Here" dot with directions may also help orient someone looking at your emergency plan.

ANNUAL LICENSE RENEWAL

1. A license is good for up to a year from the date of issue depending on the type of license issued and any provisions of it.

2. License renewal applications should be requested at least two months from the date of expiration from the DHS day care consultant.

3. The renewal forms should be filled out by the chairman of the board of the program.

4. If any changes have been made in the facilities used by the program, a new floor plan must be drawn, including measurements, and submitted.

5. The Fire Marshall's Certificate of Inspection Report must be completed annually. Contact the Fire Marshall for an appointment three months prior to the date of expiration of the current certificate to schedule an inspection appointment.

6. Contact the county Department of Health, and schedule an inspection with the Program.

RISK MANAGEMENT AND INSURANCE

Every child care program has risk. This can take the form of risk of loss to property, lawsuits or injury to employees. Before and After School Programs vary in their arrangements; each Program Board of Directors should consult with their own insurance agent for assistance in evaluating their risks and decisions regarding insurance coverage. Areas of risk include property, loss of income, extraordinary expenses, general liability, auto liability, auto liability, fidelity and injury to employees. Some exposures can be handled by insurance while others can be handled by other means of risk transfer.

Property
Most Programs have little inventory of contents and no ownership of real property (facilities). Since school facilities are utilized, there may be little need to purchase contents, other than small quantities of supplies and food. Most programs assume (self-insure) this risk. If total loss to contents is more than the program can afford, then insurance should be purchased.

Loss of Income/Extra-ordinary Expenses
Before and After School Programs are non-profit corporations. However, they still have potential exposures to loss. For example, if fire would destroy the school building, or the facilities used became unavailable owing to some emergency situation, what would happen to the Program? Do the parents make other arrangements? Which school will the children attend? Could other facilities be rented or donated to temporarily replace school facilities? Program boards should have a game plan, prior to any such actual event. If the Program board feels that it would need to incur extra ordinary expenses, then this form of insurance coverage may be considered.

General Liability
Public liability to the Program arising out of the premises and operations is a major area of concern. General Liability insurance should be used to handle this part of a Program's risk exposure. This type of insurance pays on behalf of the Program all sums it may be legally liable for to which the insurance applies, for bodily injury and property damage. Some carriers will endorse this to include the program's "professional" liability exposure. Professional coverage would cover, for example, lawsuits claiming emotional stress on the child while in the program's care. This coverage varies from company to company, therefore, the Program should consult their insurance agent for clarification on what is or is not covered.

It is important to note the exclusion that relates to property in the care of the Program, namely, the premises leased. If the Program burns down a school building, the school district's insurer will pay to rebuild, but will look for someone to sue. This risk can be effectively transferred with a waiver of "subrogation" clause in the Program's lease agreement with the school district. Essentially, this clause says that the school district and their insurer will not sue the program, if the program causes a loss to the property leased. The alternative is to buy insurance which only covers loss by fire to such property.

Automobile
Most Programs will never own an automobile, however, they probably will have someone running an errand on their behalf, using an auto. The program has a vicarious liability exposure and could be sued if a loss arises. Generally, the personal auto policy of the individual will extend the definition of "insured" to include the Program. However, the program may consider coverage of their own, called Hired and Non-Owned Auto Liability, to be assured that some coverage is afforded.

Fidelity
This exposure involves embezzlement of money and other assets by one or more employees. Much of the loss potential can be reduced with appropriate controls, for example, different people handling the deposits, check writing and bank reconciliations. The Program should again consider what it can afford to lose and how quickly they could detect a loss of this type. Insurance can be purchased, but it is relatively expensive.

Workers Compensation
State law mandates that programs carry workers compensation insurance. Officers of the corporation may elect to be excluded from coverage by signing a special form. This is commonly done to hold the cost of insurance down for organizations run by volunteer boards.

Umbrella Liability
Umbrella liability insurance is designed to protect against catastrophic liability claims. It would provide a limit of $1,000,000 or more over and above the limits of liability of other "liability" forms of insurance, such as general liability. While the cost is probably prohibitive for programs, consideration may be given.

Suggested Limits of Coverage
The limits of insurance below ar a guide for basic coverage. It is entirely possible that a judgement could exceed these limits, therefore, consideration must be given to higher limits.

Property, Loss of Income Extra-Ordinary Expenses and Crime	Program should evaluate loss potential
General Liability	$500,000 Each Occurrence $1,000,000 Aggregate $1,000 Medical Payments
Automobile Liability	$500,000 Each Occurrence
Workers Compensation Employers Liability	Statutory $500,000 Each Person $500,000 Disease $500,000 Aggregate
Umbrella Liability	$1,000,000 Combined Single Limit

Summary
Decisions concerning insurance and risk management should be made after careful consideration of all risks each program faces. Since programs will differ, the Board of Directors should consult with their insurance agent for assistance to determine if other exposures exist. It is important to maintain the insurance program after it is established, therefore, periodic reviews should be made to detect changes in risk or areas that previously may have been overlooked. Any problems then discovered should be addressed by the program at its earliest convenience.

B

BEFORE AND AFTER SCHOOL PROGRAM

BUDGETS AND PAYROLL

BUDGETS AND PAYROLL

Estimation of the costs of starting and operating a child care program is a formidable task. Factors including the number of scholarship or subsidized enrollments in the program and the wage scale in the community must be determined in order to project the budget.

Start-up budgets include many items for which money is spent prior to the collection of tuition. Large expenditures include start-up staff salaries, liability insurance, supplies, equipment, telephone installation, printing and postage. Receipts should be kept from the beginning of the start-up process for all items or services purchased. A log of the receipts and any other costs such as long distance phone calls related to the project should be kept.

A budget is both a ruler and a guide for program operation. Monthly start-up, annual expenses and income may be estimated on a ledger or "spreadsheet." By studying start-up and operating costs, those planning a program may realistically determine how much income will be needed to start and sustain it. An operating budget provides a ruler by which to measure monthly spending. It guides decisions about expenditures and encourages financial planning for the program. The budget helps programs to meet the needs and circumstances they encounter during the course of operations. Operating budget summaries are useful for providing program parents with a clear picture of program finances.

The following chapter documents the income and expenses of the fictional program, Washington Before and After School Program. The costs and items which are shown are common to a variety of programs. The budget item lists in this chapter may be modified by individual organizing committees or boards. Information about payroll related to both start-up and operating budgets is included in the later part of the chapter.

A $5,000.00 start-up grant is a part of WBASP's budget. The passage in 1990 of the new federal Child Care and Development Block Grants and reauthorization of the Dependent Care Grants means more money is available for start-up and expansion of school-age child care programs. For this reason, a comparison has been included of how a budget would be affected with and without a $5,000.00 grant.

SOURCES AND USES OF FUNDS

Annual budgets tend to grow with inflation and payroll increases. The model in this chapter is indexed to reflect this at a rate of 4% per year. If the projected expenses and number of F.T.E.'s (full time equivalents) enrolled stays the same, then budget may remain relatively stable. In the real world, however, these things are subject to change, and programs need to provide for adequate funds to cover increased expenses or lose of income.

SOURCES OF FUNDS

TYPE:	YEAR ONE		YEAR TWO	YEAR THREE
Grant	$ 5,000.00	Carryover	$ 2,481.90	$ 3,039.48
Fees	2,060.00		200.00	200.00
Tuition	30,240.00		30,240.00	30,240.00
INCOME	**$37,300.00**		**$32,921.90**	**$33,479.48**

Year One: Finding opportunities for forming program capital is crucial at program outset. Start-up grants may be available through state departments of education or human services, or through employers and community resources. Additional funds may also be developed through the implementation of non-refundable registration and enrollment fees (see Form Book).
Years Two and Three: Years two and three may be lean on opportunities to fund expenses in other ways than tuition. Tuition is entered above as stable.

USES OF FUNDS

TYPE:	YEAR ONE	YEAR TWO	YEAR THREE
Start-Up 1st Year	$ 3,585.00		
Start-Up	2,295.00	$ 2,386.80	$ 2,482.27
Operating	26,438.10	27,495.62	28,595.45
Contingency	2,500.00	1,000.00	1,000.00
EXPENSES	**$34,818.10**	**$29,882.42**	**$31,077.72**

Year One: Year One has two entries labeled as start-up expenses. Start-Up 1st Year expenses are incurred at the outset of a program's first year. A breakdown of these costs may be found later in this chapter. The second start up entry in Year One is the cost of second year start-up for which funds must be accrued during Year One. It is well to plan for a contingency fund at the outset of a program, and provide for carryover of some of those funds.
Year Two and Three: Years Two and Three show increasing operating expenses and accrual of next year start-up and contingency funds. After Year One, each successive year shown has been indexed by 4% to provide for inflation and pay increases.

CASH FLOW

The following figures show an overall picture of cash flow for three years, using the figures established on the previous page, Sources and Uses of Funds.

YEAR ONE

$ 0.00	Beginning Balance for Year One
5,000.00	Grant
32,300.00	Total Fees, Tuition Income
$37,300.00	**Total First Year Income**
- 3,585.00	Minus First Year Start-Up Expenses
-26,438.10	Minus First Year Operating Expenses
$ 7,276.90	**Ending Balance for Year One**

In the first year, as in every year, program funds must be accumulated so that they will be sufficient to pay expenses, leaving enough in the balance to pay for next year's start-up.

YEAR TWO

$ 7,276.90	Beginning Balance for Year Two
30,440.00	Total Fees and Tuition Income
37,716.90	**Total Second Year Income + Carryover**
- 2,295.00	Minus Second Year Start-Up Expenses
-27,495.62	Minus Second Year Operating Expenses
$ 7,926.28	**Ending Balance for Year Two**

Both Income and Expenses may drop in the second year of operation.

YEAR THREE

$ 7,926.28	Beginning Balance for Year Three
30,440.00	Total Fees and Tuition Income
$38,366.28	**Total Third Year Income + Carryover**
- 2,482.27	Minus Third Year Start-Up Expenses
-28,595.45	Minus Third Year Operating Expenses
$ 7,288.56	**Ending Balance for Year Three**

Income and Expenses may stabilize in the third year, unless the program decides to expand.

FIRST YEAR START-UP EXPENSES

First year start-up expenses are necessarily high. They include a number of one-time-only items which include filing fees, telephone installation and permanent equipment.

Fees: **$405.00**
$ 20.00	Filing Fee for Articles of Incorporation
25.00	Filing Fee for County Articles of Incorporation
300.00	Filing Fee for Tax Exempt Status (in first year)
(donated)	Legal Fee for Articles of Incorporation and Bylaws
40.00	Health Department Inspection (if applicable)
20.00	Toy Lending Library

Insurance: **$1,100.00**
$1,100.00	Liability Insurance and Workers Compensation

Equipment: **$525.00**
$ 125.00	Telephone and Extension Installation Charge
100.00	Used Refrigerator
50.00	Used Storage Cabinet
250.00	Files and Office Supplies

Staff: **$600.00**
$ 100.00	Classified Advertising for Staff
400.00	Director's Salary for Start-Up Period
80.00	Payroll Taxes
20.00	Staff First Aid Training

Professional Resources: **$135.00**
$ 35.00	NAEYC Membership
100.00	Professional Resources

Supplies & Equipment: **$820.00**
$ 20.00	First Aid Kit
100.00	Printing
30.00	Postage
20.00	Checks
400.00	Activity equipment and toys
150.00	First month food
100.00	Food Service Equipment and Supplies
TOTAL =	**$3,585.00**

FIRST YEAR START-UP INCOME

The Program will have a number of financial responsibilities prior to the receipt of first month tuition. In order to provide for these expenses, start-up income must be developed from a combination of registration and enrollment fees as well as additional funding shown here as a $5,000.00 grant.

START-UP INCOME:

$ 800.00	Registration fee ($20.00 X 40 families)
1,260.00	Enrollment fee ($35.00 X 36 children)
5,000.00	Grant money
	Donations and In-Kind Services
$7,060.00	**Total Start Up Income**

1. START-UP SCENARIO WITH A $5000.00 GRANT:

In this scenario, fees along with a substantial grant will meet start-up expenses and extend into the first month's budget. This is a favorable start.

$	7,060.00	Total Start Up Income Including Grant
	-3,585.00	Total First Year Start Up Expenses
$	**3,475.00**	**Carryover**

2. START-UP SCENARIO NO GRANT:

It is clear that lack of start-up funding creates a deficit as shown by the shortfall shown above. This start-up scenario anticipates that higher fees will replace the shortfall.

$	2,060.00	Total Start Up Income Excluding Grant
	-3,585.00	Total First Year Start Up Expenses
$	**-1,525.00**	**Shortfall**

First year start-up is more expensive than annual start-up thereafter. The financial challenge posed by first year start-up expenses must be met by a concerted effort to obtain the needed funds. If governmental grant funds are not available, development of funding from other sources will be needed. Local employers, churches and civic groups may be able to participate in forming the capital needed for a BASP project.

ANNUAL START-UP EXPENSES
AFTER THE FIRST YEAR

The annual start up budget after the first year is detailed below. These figures may be indexed in each successive year by 4% to anticipate growth due to inflation and pay increases.

ANNUAL START-UP EXPENSES AFTER THE FIRST YEAR:

Fees: **$60.00**
$ 40.00   Health Department inspection fee (if applicable
    20.00   Lending Library

Insurance: **$1,100.00**
$1,100.00   Liability Insurance and Workers Compensation

Staff: **$600.00**
$ 100.00   Classified Advertising for Staff
    400.00   Director's Salary (for work over the interim)
     80.00   Payroll Taxes
    20.00   Staff First Aid Training

Professional
Resources: **$35.00**
$ 35.00   NAEYC Membership

Supplies and
Equipment: **$500.00**
$ 50.00   Files and Office Supplies
    20.00   First Aid Kit (restock)
  100.00   Printing
    30.00   Postage
  100.00   Activity Equipment and Toys
  150.00   First Month Food
    50.00   Food Service Equipment and Supplies

TOTAL   **$2,295.00 Second Year**
Indexed by 4%   **$2,386.80 Third Year**
Indexed by 4%   **$2,482.27 Fourth Year**

ANNUAL OPERATING EXPENSES

The annual operating budget is detailed below. These figures may be indexed in each successive year by 5% to anticipate growth due to inflation and pay increases.

ANNUAL OPERATING EXPENSES:

Personnel:	**$22,838.10**
$10,000.00	Director Salary
1,225.00	Director Payroll Taxes
9,900.00	Aide Salaries (two aides: $4,950.00 X 2)
1,363.10	Aide Payroll Taxes ($681.55 x 2)
100.00	Bookkeeper or Accountant for payroll and taxes
250.00	Substitute Personnel
Equipment:	**$400.00**
$ 400.00	Activity Program Toys & Equipment
Supplies:	**$450.00**
$ 300.00	Activity Program
150.00	Administrative (Including printing)
Food:	**$2,000.00**
$2,000.00	Breakfast and Afternoon Snack
Professional	
Resources:	**$400.00**
$ 150.00	Professional Resources and Training
250.00	Conference Expense
Other:	**$300.00**
$ 50.00	Classified Advertising

TOTAL =	**$26,438.10 First Year**
Indexed by 4%	**$27,495.62 Second Year**
Indexed by 4%	**$28,595.45 Third Year**

TUITION CALCULATION

The operational budget should be self-sustaining, accrue enough funds to cover start up during the next year, as well as develop a contingency fund. Additionally, enough funds should be available to cover an increase in expenses or loss of income. The following illustration demonstrates the impact of a start-up grant. Contrast tuition affordability in the examples. Hourly rates are $1.25 and $1.45 per hour in these examples given.

1. Year 1 Low Example (With Grant)

First Year Start Up Expenses	$ 3,585.00
First Year Operating Expenses	26,438.10
Second Year Start Up Expenses	2,295.00
Contingency Fund	2,500.00
Total First Year Budget	**$34,818.10**
Minus Start Up Income:	-2,060.00
Minus Start Up Grant:	-5,000.00
Tuition Supported Budget	**$27,758.10**

Tuition Calculation: 30 FTE's X 22.5 hours per week = 675 Hours of care
675 hours of care X 36 weeks = 24,300 hours of care/year
$27,758.10 divided by 24,300 hours = **$1.14 per hour** rate (with grant)
Round this up to $1.25 per hour.
22.5 hours/week X $1.25 = $28.13/week
Round this down to $28.00
$28.00/week X 4 weeks = **$112.00/month full time**
$108.00 x 9 months = **$1,008.00 Annual Tuition**
$1,008.00 Annual Tuition X 30 FTE's = $30,240.00

2. Year 1 High Example (<u>Without</u> Grant)

First Year Start Up Expenses:	$ 3,585.00
First Year Operating Expenses:	26,438.10
Second Year Start Up Expenses:	2,295.00
Contingency Fund	2,500.00
Total First Year Budget	**$34,818.10**
Minus Start Up Income:	-2,060.00
Tuition Supported Budget	**$32,758.10**

Tuition Calculation: 30 FTE's X 22.5 hours per week = 675 Hours of care
675 hours of care X 36 weeks = 24,300 hours of care/year
$32,758.10 divided by 24,300 hours = **$1.35/hour rate** <u>without</u> grant
The $1.35/hour figure might well be raised to $1.45.
22.5 hours/week X $1.35 = $32.63 X 4 weeks = **$130.52/month full time**
$130.52 X 9 months = **$1,174.68 Annual Tuition**
$1,093.68 X 30 FTE's = $32,810.40

SALARY CALCULATION

GROSS SALARY CALCULATION:

Child Care Director:

$10.00 per hour x 25 hours per week = $250.00

x 40 weeks (36 week school year plus 4 additional weeks) = $10,000.00 Gross Salary

Divided by 9 months = $1,111.00 Gross Monthly Salary

Child Care Aides:

$5.50 per hour x 25 hours per week = $137.50

x 36 weeks = $4,950.00 Gross Salary

Divided by 9 months = $550.00 Gross Monthly Salary

EMPLOYEE'S SALARY DEDUCTIONS:

Net salaries are calculated by deducting the following from the gross amount:

FICA - Employee's share of social security = .0751 of gross
Federal Withholdings - figured on a Federal W-4 form
State Withholdings - figured on a State W-4 form

EMPLOYER-PAID ITEMS:

The following salary budget items which are paid by the employer and may not be deducted from the employee's salary include:

FICA - Employer's share of social security = .0751 of gross
FUTA - Federal Unemployment Tax = .062 of the first $7000 of salary
State Unemployment Tax = a low rate, in Iowa it is .0006 up to $11,500

Each child care program also must purchase Workers Compensation insurance. It is purchased privately, usually together with liability insurance.

PAYROLL BUDGET CALCULATION

1.　NET SALARIES

Employee's net salaries are calculated by subtracting deductions from the gross. Deductions are made on a monthly basis. For example:

Salary	ANNUAL	MONTHLY (divide by 9)
Gross:	$10,000.00	$1,100.00
FICA	751.00	83.44
Fed W/H	900.00	100.00
State W/H	170.00	19.00
NET:	$8,179.00	$908.56

2.　EMPLOYER PAID ITEMS

The salary section of a Program budget also should include payments which are not deducted from the employee's salary:

FICA - Employer's share of social security = .0751 of gross
FUTA - Federal Unemployment Tax = .062 of the first $7000
State Unemployment Tax = .0006 up to $11,500

Child Care Director:

Employer Paid Taxes	ANNUAL	QUARTERLY	MONTHLY
FICA	$751.00	$187.75	$83.44
FUTA	434.00	108.22	48.22
State Unemployment	6.00	1.50	.66
TOTAL	$1,191.00	$297.47	$132.32

Aide:

Employer Paid Taxes	ANNUAL	QUARTERLY	MONTHLY
FICA	$371.75	$92.94	$41.31
FUTA	306.90	76.73	34.10
State Unemployment	2.90	.73	.32
TOTAL	$681.55	$170.40	$75.73

TAXES: STATE & FEDERAL

Figuring out taxes is can be difficult and time consuming. It is necessary to have an accountant or an attorney to guide programs through this process. Some organizers find that they have parents of potential program children who will volunteer their professional skills. If a parent/professional/volunteer is not available, programs should to employ someone for tax and payroll services.

FEDERAL

Programs need to apply for a Federal identification number. This is often referred to as your "42" number. It enables the organization to withhold tax. Your organization will hereafter be known on tax information by your 42 number. To request a form you will phone the IRS number, 1-800-424-3676, and request an SS-4 application for a Federal ID number or contact an attorney or tax preparer. At that time, you should also request the following forms.

W-4 - This is the form on which your employees will figure their Federal withholdings. You will need one for each staff person and substitute whom you employ.

W-2 - These are the end-of-the-year Federal tax forms for your employees. You will need one for each staff person and substitute whom you employ.

W-3 - This is the end-of-the-year employers transmittal form for reporting of the information on wages and withholding.

W-10- Dependent Care Provider's Identification and Certification

940 - (FUTA) Federal Unemployment Tax form (paid quarterly)

941 - (FICA) Federal Social Security Tax form (paid quarterly)

1023- Application for Tax Exempt Status (large filing fee if you choose to do this)

1120- Regular Federal corporation income tax form -or-

990 - Non-profit, tax-exempt corporation income tax form. (You will not use this form unless you have applied for tax-exempt status and filed the 1023 application and have received your tax-exempt letter.

STATE

Using your Federal ID (42) number, you will register with the State Department of Revenue and request your withholding forms and instruction booklet. They usually come with a coupon booklet. The coupons accompany payment. At that time you will also request:

State W-4 - State withholdings tax form. You will need one for all employees and substitutes.

State W-2 - State end-of-the-year form for both employers and staff.

State corporation income tax form -or-

State non-profit, tax-exempt income tax form

Annual Withholding Agent Verified Summary of Payments Report

State Unemployment Tax form (from state Job Services office

BEFORE AND AFTER SCHOOL PROGRAM

TUITION DUE NOTICE

We have not received your tuition payment for the month of _____, which was due on _____. The Program salaries, supplies and administrative expenses are supported entirely by fees. In accordance with our policies stated in the Parent Handbook, we are requesting immediate payment. Please contact the Program Treasurer regarding any financial concerns related to tuition. All concerns expressed to the Board will be kept confidential within the confines of the Board of Directors.

_____
Treasurer, Before and After School Program
Board of Directors

Before and After School Operating Budget

EXPENSES	AUG	SEP	OCT	NOV	DEC	JAN	FEB	MAR	APR	MAY	JUN	JUL	TOTAL
Personnel:													
Director	$____	$____	$____	$____	$____	$____	$____	$____	$____	$____	$____	$____	$____
FICA	$____	$____	$____	$____	$____	$____	$____	$____	$____	$____	$____	$____	$____
FUTA	$____	$____	$____	$____	$____	$____	$____	$____	$____	$____	$____	$____	$____
State Unempl.	$____	$____	$____	$____	$____	$____	$____	$____	$____	$____	$____	$____	$____
Aide 1	$____	$____	$____	$____	$____	$____	$____	$____	$____	$____	$____	$____	$____
FICA	$____	$____	$____	$____	$____	$____	$____	$____	$____	$____	$____	$____	$____
FUTA	$____	$____	$____	$____	$____	$____	$____	$____	$____	$____	$____	$____	$____
State Unempl.	$____	$____	$____	$____	$____	$____	$____	$____	$____	$____	$____	$____	$____
Aide 2	$____	$____	$____	$____	$____	$____	$____	$____	$____	$____	$____	$____	$____
FICA	$____	$____	$____	$____	$____	$____	$____	$____	$____	$____	$____	$____	$____
FUTA	$____	$____	$____	$____	$____	$____	$____	$____	$____	$____	$____	$____	$____
State Unempl	$____	$____	$____	$____	$____	$____	$____	$____	$____	$____	$____	$____	$____
Bookkeeper	$____	$____	$____	$____	$____	$____	$____	$____	$____	$____	$____	$____	$____
Substitute	$____	$____	$____	$____	$____	$____	$____	$____	$____	$____	$____	$____	$____
FICA	$____	$____	$____	$____	$____	$____	$____	$____	$____	$____	$____	$____	$____
FUTA	$____	$____	$____	$____	$____	$____	$____	$____	$____	$____	$____	$____	$____
State Unempl.	$____	$____	$____	$____	$____	$____	$____	$____	$____	$____	$____	$____	$____
Insurance:													
Liability	$____	$____	$____	$____	$____	$____	$____	$____	$____	$____	$____	$____	$____
Worker's Compensation	$____	$____	$____	$____	$____	$____	$____	$____	$____	$____	$____	$____	$____
Occupancy:													
Telephone	$____	$____	$____	$____	$____	$____	$____	$____	$____	$____	$____	$____	$____
Equipment:													
Activity Program	$____	$____	$____	$____	$____	$____	$____	$____	$____	$____	$____	$____	$____
Food Service	$____	$____	$____	$____	$____	$____	$____	$____	$____	$____	$____	$____	$____
Housekeeping	$____	$____	$____	$____	$____	$____	$____	$____	$____	$____	$____	$____	$____
Administration	$____	$____	$____	$____	$____	$____	$____	$____	$____	$____	$____	$____	$____

Before and After School Operating Budget (Continued)

	AUG	SEP	OCT	NOV	DEC	JAN	FEB	MAR	APR	MAY	JUN	JUL	TOTAL
Supplies:													
Activity Program	$	$	$	$	$	$	$	$	$	$	$	$	$
Food Service	$	$	$	$	$	$	$	$	$	$	$	$	$
Housekeeping	$	$	$	$	$	$	$	$	$	$	$	$	$
Administration	$	$	$	$	$	$	$	$	$	$	$	$	$
Food:													
Snacks	$	$	$	$	$	$	$	$	$	$	$	$	$
Other Expenses:													
Loan Repayment	$	$	$	$	$	$	$	$	$	$	$	$	$
NAEYC Membership	$	$	$	$	$	$	$	$	$	$	$	$	$
Toy Lending	$	$	$	$	$	$	$	$	$	$	$	$	$
Subscriptions	$	$	$	$	$	$	$	$	$	$	$	$	$
Advertising	$	$	$	$	$	$	$	$	$	$	$	$	$
Total Expenses:	$	$	$	$	$	$	$	$	$	$	$	$	$
INCOME													
Tuition	$	$	$	$	$	$	$	$	$	$	$	$	$
In-Kind	$	$	$	$	$	$	$	$	$	$	$	$	$
Donations	$	$	$	$	$	$	$	$	$	$	$	$	$
Fundraising	$	$	$	$	$	$	$	$	$	$	$	$	$
Other	$	$	$	$	$	$	$	$	$	$	$	$	$
Total Income	$	$	$	$	$	$	$	$	$	$	$	$	$
Balance	$	$	$	$	$	$	$	$	$	$	$	$	$

BEFORE AND AFTER SCHOOL PROGRAM

APPLICATION FOR TAX-EXEMPT STATUS

APPLICATION FOR TAX-EXEMPT STATUS

Few organizational activities incite anxieties like the process of applying for recognition of exemption. None-the-less, it is preferable to conquer discomfort and complete the form rather than pay annual corporation taxes. The one-time application fee is often in the range of a year's tax payment.

Section 501(c)(3) of the Internal Revenue Code

Section 501(c)(3) of the Internal Revenue Code provides that the provision of day care services will be considered educational for its purposes if 1) the care is provided to enable the childrens' parent(s) to be gainfully employed, attend school or seek employment, and 2) that services are provided to the general public.

Time Frame for Application

It is recommended that programs apply for exemption within the first fifteen months of program operation. Instructions for the 1023 state that for a program to be eligible to receive a definitive (final) ruling, an organization must have completed a tax year of at least 8 months. However, programs should hold off on filing the application until they can provide a year-end statement for their first fiscal year.

Steps in the Application Process

1. **Forms 1023, Form 8718** (user fee), **Publication 557** (additional instructions), and **Form 8718** (User fee for Exempt Organization Determination Letter Request) may be ordered from the Internal Revenue Service (IRS) by phone: 1-800-424-3676. Forms will arrive approximately 10 days after the request. Check with your state's Department of Revenue and Finance for any necessary forms regarding exemption from state corporation income tax.

2. Obtain a copies of information to attach to the 1023 application including:

    1. The program's fee and tuition schedule

    2. The program's nondiscriminatory enrollment policy

    3. The Parent Handbook

4.   The number of children in the program whose enrollment allow the parent(s) to be gainfully employed, attend school or seek employment

5.   How you inform the general public that the services you provide are open to the general public. Provide copies of appropriate brochures, flyers and newspaper advertisements.

6.   The number of minority group children enrolled

7.   Scholarship and subsidized enrollments, governmental and private

8.   The space agreement with the school

9.   A breakdown of any grant money received according to the type of program expenses covered (ie: salaries, insurance, equipment, etc.)

10.   A list of depreciable and depletable assets

11.   Copies of the program's current bylaws and the articles of incorporation which have been signed by the board of directors and display the seal of approval by the Secretary of State.

12.   A year-end income/expenses statement

13.   Projected budgets for the next two years of program operations

3.   When the application forms arrive, photocopy (or obtain multiple copies) so that a "clean" copy may be used for the final draft which will be submitted to the IRS. The application booklet will contain only two copies of each application form.

4.   If the program's annual information return becomes due while you application is pending, you should file **Form 990** (Return of Organization Exempt From Income Tax) by the 15th day of the 5th month after the end of your accounting period. Copies of Form 990 may be used to satisfy state reporting requirements; this should be checked with an office of the state Internal Revenue Service.

Upon the arrival of the forms, the board president and treasurer together with legal counsel or other designated persons will undertake to complete the forms.

After the program has received the letter granting federal tax-exemption, it must immediately apply for state tax exemption. This process is generally facilitated by and dependent upon the prior receipt of a federal definitive ruling.

WASHINGTON BEFORE AND AFTER SCHOOL PROGRAM
BACKGROUND

Washington Before and After School Program WBASP has been in operation for one fiscal year. The program operates every school day from 7 to 8:30 am and 3:00 to 6:00 pm, utilizing the gym, two kindergarten rooms, kitchen and two bathrooms of Washington Elementary School. At other times these facilities are also regularly used by a number of organizations including Scouts, Camp Fire, P.T.A., and aerobics and foreign language classes.

WBASP was started by a committee of Washington parents who, in cooperation with the school principal, developed and implemented the program. The mission of the program is to provide quality, accessible, affordable, developmentally appropriate child care for children in grades K-6, so that their parents can be gainfully employed, attend school or seek employment.

WBASP is open to the public. It is willing to enroll children from other schools, however this has not occured since every elementary school in the River City School District has a before and after school program.

WBASP does not discriminate on the basis of sex, race, color, disability, creed, national origin or ethnic background.

The Program has its employer identification number (42) and is non-profit incorporated. The Board applied for a $5,000.00 State Department of Human Services Child Day Care Grant start up grant, which was fully funded. This was a one-time grant program.

WBASP intends to be a self-supporting center which will derive its operational support primarily from fees assessed the parents of the children who are registered and enrolled. Since all of the parents are working full time and have limited time for fund raising, they have elected to cover their expenses primarily with fees.

The following fictional forms demonstrate WBASP's application for recognition of exemption.

FORM 8718

Across from this page please direct your attention to the one page Form 8718. On this form the fee for the type of request will be indicated.

Washington Before and After School Program has checked box B since the program's annual income will exceed $10,000.00 annually. They will submit their $300.00 check attached to the indicated section of this form.

Form **8718**
(Rev. January 1989)
Department of the Treasury
Internal Revenue Service

User Fee for Exempt Organization Determination Letter Request

▶ Attach to determination letter applications.

1 Name of organization   Washington Before & After School Program

2   Type of request (check only one box and include a check or money order made payable to Internal Revenue Service for the amount of the indicated fee):

Fee

a ☐   Initial request for recognition of tax-exempt status under section 501(a) (except a section 401(a) trust) by an organization whose gross receipts have not exceeded (or are not expected to exceed) $10,000 annually, averaged over its first four taxable years. If you check this box you must complete the income certification below . . . . $ 150

Certification

I hereby certify that the gross receipts of _____ have not exceeded (or are not
                                                                    (enter name of organization)

expected to exceed) $10,000 annually, averaged over its first four years of operation.

Signature ▶ _____ Title   President, Board of Directors

b X   All other initial requests for recognition of tax-exempt status under section 501(a) or 521 (except a section 401(a) trust)   .   .   .   . $ 300

c ☐   Private foundation which has completed a section 507 termination and which seeks a determination letter that it is now a public charity.   .   .   .   . $ 200

Instructions

The Revenue Act of 1987 requires payment of a user fee for determination letter requests submitted to the Internal Revenue Service. The fee must accompany each request submitted to a key district office.

The fee for each type of request for an exempt organization determination letter is listed in item 2 of this form. Check the block that describes the type of request you are submitting, and attach this form to the front of your request form along with a check or money order for the amount indicated. Make the check or money order payable to the Internal Revenue Service.

Determination letter requests received with no payment or with an insufficient payment will be returned to the applicant for submission of the proper fee. To avoid delays in receiving a determination letter,

be sure that your application is sent to the applicable address shown below. These addresses supersede the addresses listed in Publication 557 and all application forms.

If entity is in this IRS District ▼	Send fee and request for determination letter to this address ▼
Brooklyn, Albany, Augusta, Boston, Buffalo, Burlington, Hartford, Manhattan, Portsmouth, Providence	Internal Revenue Service EP/EO Division P. O. Box 1680, GPO Brooklyn, NY 11202
Baltimore, District of Columbia, Pittsburgh, Richmond, Newark, Philadelphia, Wilmington, any U.S. possession or foreign country	Internal Revenue Service EP/EO Division P. O. Box 17010 Baltimore, MD 21203
Cincinnati, Cleveland, Detroit, Indianapolis, Louisville, Parkersburg	Internal Revenue Service EP/EO Division P. O. Box 3159 Cincinnati, OH 45201
Dallas, Albuquerque, Austin, Cheyenne, Denver, Houston, Oklahoma City, Phoenix, Salt Lake City, Wichita	Internal Revenue Service EP/EO Division Mail Code 4950 DAL 1100 Commerce Street Dallas, TX 75242
Atlanta, Birmingham, Columbia, Ft. Lauderdale, Greensboro, Jackson, Jacksonville, Little Rock, Nashville, New Orleans	Internal Revenue Service EP/EO Division C-1130 Atlanta, GA 30301
Anchorage, Las Vegas, Boise, Los Angeles, Honolulu, Portland, Laguna Niguel, San Jose, Seattle	Internal Revenue Service EO Application Receiving Room 5127, P. O. Box 486 Los Angeles, CA 90053-0486
Sacramento, San Francisco	Internal Revenue Service EO Application Receiving Stop SF 4446 P. O. Box 36001 San Francisco, CA 94102
Chicago, Aberdeen, Des Moines, Fargo, Helena, Milwaukee, Omaha, St. Louis, St. Paul, Springfield	Internal Revenue Service EP/EO Division 230 S. Dearborn DPN 20-5 Chicago, IL 60604

Attach Check or Money Order Here

FORM 1023

Form 1023 is a lengthy form which is found bound together with its instructions in a booklet. Two copies of each application page are provided back-to-back in the booklet.

Pages 1-6 of the 1023 booklet contain instructions for each section of the application. Additional information is supplied in Publication 557.

Page 7 of the 1023 booklet displays a list of "red flag" components of the form which must be supplied to complete the application. This is a handy list. Use it as a checklist prior to filing.

Page 1

Part I. Identification of Applicant

WBASP has entered its:

1a.   Legal name
1b.   Name of Board President
1c.   Address
1d.   City, state and ZIP code

2.   Employer Identification Number
3.   Name and telephone number of the Board President
4.   Month the accounting year ends
5.   Date of incorporation
6.   Activity code (574 = Day Care Center)
7.   Applicant section 501(k) (Organization Providing Child Care)

8-9.   WBASP has indicated "no" to numbers 8 and 9 since this will be its first application for exemption and its has not filed any income tax returns.

10.   WBASP has checked "Corporation" and will attach copies of their stamped Articles of Incorporation and bylaws.

Form **1023** (Rev. December 1989) Department of the Treasury Internal Revenue Service	**Application for Recognition of Exemption** **Under Section 501(c)(3) of the Internal Revenue Code**	OMB No. 1545-0056 If exempt status is approved, this application will be open for public inspection.

Read the instructions for each Part carefully.
A User Fee must be attached to this application.

If the required information and appropriate documents are not submitted along with Form 8718 (with payment of the appropriate user fee), the application may be returned to you.

Part I   Identification of Applicant

1a Full name of organization (as shown in organizing document) Washington Before & After School Child Care Program	**2** Employer identification number **(If none, see instructions.)** 42-123456

1b c/o Name (if applicable)	**3** Name and telephone number of person to be contacted if additional information is needed Kathleen Berg (531) 243-4331

1c Address (number and street) 2000 Lakeside Drive	( )

1d City or town, state, and ZIP code River City, Iowa 52248	**4** Month the annual accounting period ends June 30

5 Date incorporated or formed April 30, 1989	**6** Activity codes (See instructions.) 574		**7** Check here if applying under section: a ☐ 501(e) b ☐ 501(f) X 501(k)

8 Did the organization previously apply for recognition of exemption under this Code section or under any other section of the Code? . . . . ☐ **Yes**   X **No**
If "Yes," attach an explanation.

9 Has the organization filed Federal income tax returns or exempt organization information returns? . . . . . ☐ **Yes**   X **No**
If "Yes," state the form number(s), years filed, and Internal Revenue office where filed.

10 Check the box for your type of organization. BE SURE TO ATTACH A COMPLETE COPY OF THE CORRESPONDING DOCUMENTS TO THE APPLICATION BEFORE MAILING.

a X Corporation— Attach a copy of your Articles of Incorporation, (including amendments and restatements) showing approval by the appropriate state official; also include a copy of your bylaws.

b ☐ Trust— Attach a copy of your Trust Indenture or Agreement, including all appropriate signatures and dates.

c ☐ Association— Attach a copy of your Articles of Association, Constitution, or other creating document, with a declaration (see instructions) or other evidence the organization was formed by adoption of the document by more than one person; also include a copy of your bylaws.

If you are a corporation or an unincorporated association that has not yet adopted bylaws, check here . . . . ▶ ☐

I declare under the penalties of perjury that I am authorized to sign this application on behalf of the above organization and that I have examined this application, including the accompanying schedules and attachments, and to the best of my knowledge it is true, correct, and complete.

Please Sign Here ▶		President, Board of Directors	July 1, 1990
	(Signature)	(Title or authority of signer)	(Date)

For Paperwork Reduction Act Notice, see page 1 of the instructions.

Complete the Procedural Checklist (page 7 of the instructions) prior to filing.

Part II.   Activities and Organizational Information

1.   WBASP has provided an account of WBASP's past, present and proposed future activities contained in a narrative description of the program. Enough information is given for the reader to have an accurate view of the program's status.

2.   WBASP has listed in order from largest to smallest, its sources of program income. They will attach their fee schedule to the application in order to demonstrate the amounts of these fees.

3.   WBASP has described its funding plan.

Part II   **Activities and Operational Information**

1   Provide a detailed narrative description of all the activities of the organization—past, present, and planned. **Do not merely refer to or repeat the language in your organizational document.** Describe each activity separately in the order of importance. Each description should include, as a minimum, the following: (a) a detailed description of the activity including its purpose; (b) when the activity was or will be initiated; and (c) where and by whom the activity will be conducted.

Washington Before and After School Program (WBASP) has been providing child care for one fiscal year. The program operates every school day from 7 to 8:30 am and 3:00 to 6:00 pm, utilizing the gym, playground, two kindergarten rooms, kitchen and two bathrooms of Washington Elementary School. At other times these facilities are also regularly used by a number of organizations including Scouts, Camp Fire, P.T.A., and aerobics and foreign language classes. WBASP is administered by a board of directors, implemented by the Child Care Director, and is affiliated with the school by means of a space agreement. The school's principal is a member of the board of directors. It is an Iowa non-profit corporation organized pursuant to Chapter 504A, 1989 Code of Iowa, and is licensed under the regulations of the Iowa Department of Human Services (DHS). WBASP was started by a committee of Washington parents in cooperation with the school principal. The mission of the program is to provide accessible, affordable, developmentally appropriate child care for children in grades K-6, so that their parents can be gainfully employed, attend school or seek employment. WBASP is open to the public; it does not discriminate on the basis of sex, race, color, disability, creed, national origin or ethnic background. The program offers a variety of activities for children, and provides a safe, friendly environment. The Child Care Director is assisted by aides; together they supervise the children's activities. Additionally, the director plans activities, registers and enrolls children, and maintains childrens' and staff files in compliance with licensing regulations. Activities include games, sports, arts and crafts, movies, and a daily breakfast and afternoon snack. Occasionally a special resource person (artist, magician, etc.) provides a presentation. A summary of organizational activities includes:

January - March 1989: Needs assessment survey of Washington School families, formation of a committee of parent volunteers (later to become the board of directors), committee consultation with the day care consultant from the state licensing agency regarding facilities and procedures for starting a child care program.

April - June 1989: WBASP became a non-profit corporation, staff were hired, a budget was drawn up, equipment was assembled, registrations and enrollments were solicited for 1990-91 school year.

July - August 1989: The board applied for a start-up loan from the Department of Human Services, liability insurance was purchased, government payroll forms were prepared.

August 29, 1989: The program officially began operation.

Future activities of the program include the continued operation of the program, with the possibility of raising enrollment from the present 30 FTE's to 35. The program would like to acquire additional materials and equipment for the use of the children, and increase staffing to improve the child-adult ratio as funds allow.

2   What are or will be the organization's sources of financial support? List in order of size.

1. Monthly tuition payments from parents of children enrolled
2. Nonrefundable enrollment fees
3. Nonrefundable registration fees (see fee schedule)

3   Describe the organization's fundraising program, both actual and planned, and explain to what extent it has been put into effect. (Include details of fundraising activities such as selective mailings, formation of fundraising committees, use of volunteers or professional fundraisers, etc.) Attach representative copies of solicitations for financial support.

WBASP intends to be a self-supporting, nonprofit child care center which will derive its operational support primarily from fees and tuition. Since all of the childrens' parents are working full time, and have limited time for fundraising, they have decided to cover expenses in this manner. (see 1989-90 Year-End Statement)

4a.   WBASP has listed its Board officers, and has indicated (b.) that they are not provided any compensation for service.

c.   The elementary school principal is the only member of the Board who is a public official.

d.   WBASP has no "disqualified persons."

5.   WBASP is self-governing (No) and does not have a relationship with another organization (No).

6.   WBASP does not plan to engage in transactions with any of the entities listed (No).

7.   WBASP is not financially accountable to any other organization.

Part II   Activities and Operational Information *(Continued)*

4   Give the following information about the organization's governing body:

a Names, addresses, and titles of officers, directors, trustees, etc.	**b** Annual Compensation
President: Kathleen Berg 2345 Gleason Ave. River City, Iowa 52248 Secretary: Danielle Holden 3728 Benny Court River City, Iowa 52248 Treasurer: Ann Hill 1507 Kelly Lane River City, Iowa 52248 Donna Walker 4507 Crosby River City, Iowa 52248 Alan Kindhart 3476 Hope Drive River City, Iowa 52248 Principal: Paul McDonald 2801 Astair Road River City, Iowa 52248	No compensation

c   Do any of the above persons serve as members of the governing body by reason of being public officials or being appointed by public officials? . . . . **X** **Yes**   ☐ **No**
If "Yes," name those persons and explain the basis of their selection or appointment.

The principal of the elementary school which houses the program is always a member of the board.

d   Are any members of the organization's governing body "disqualified persons" with respect to the organization (other than by reason of being a member of the governing body) or do any of the members have either a business or family relationship with "disqualified persons"? (See the Specific Instructions for line 4d.) . . . . ☐ **Yes**   **X** **No**
If "Yes," explain.

5   Does the organization control or is it controlled by any other organization? . . . . ☐ **Yes**   **X** **No**
Is the organization the outgrowth of (or successor to) another organization, or does it have a special relationship to another organization by reason of interlocking directorates or other factors? . . . . ☐ **Yes**   **X** **No**
If either of these questions is answered "Yes," explain.

6   Does or will the organization directly or indirectly engage in any of the following transactions with any political organization or other exempt organization (other than 501(c)(3) organizations): (a) grants; (b) purchases or sales of assets; (c) rental of facilities or equipment; (d) loans or loan guarantees; (e) reimbursement arrangements; (f) performance of services, membership, or fundraising solicitations; or (g) sharing of facilities, equipment, mailing lists or other assets, or paid employees? . . . . ☐ **Yes**   **X** **No**
If "Yes," explain fully and identify the other organization(s) involved.

7   Is the organization financially accountable to any other organization? . . . . ☐ **Yes**   **X** **No**
If "Yes," explain and identify the other organization. Include details concerning accountability or attach copies of reports if any have been submitted.

8.   Since all of WBASPs property is used to carry out the program, it is briefly mentioned.

9a.   WBASP does not "contract out" any of its "operation." Those persons who carry out the program are employees of the Board of Directors under employment contracts.

9b.   WBASP is not a party to any lease.

10.   WBASP is not a membership organization in the sense of fees and dues paying members. Registration, enrollment and tuition fees are paid for services provided rather than for membership benefits.

11a. WBASP provides child care services (Yes). A fee income schedule has been attached to provide information about this.

11b. WBASP has indicated that its services are provided to children in grades K-6 (Yes).

12.   WBASP does not plan to lobby (No).

13.   WBASP does not plan to engage in political campaign activities (No).

Part II   **Activities and Operational Information** *(Continued)*

8   What assets does the organization have that are used in the performance of its exempt function? (Do not include property producing investment income.) If any assets are not fully operational, explain their status, what additional steps remain to be completed, and when such final steps will be taken. If "None," indicate "N/A."

All of the program's assets are used in the performance of its exempt function; they include:
A used storage cabinet, a used refrigerator, toys and games, arts and crafts supplies, office supplies

9a   Will any of the organization's facilities or operations be managed by another organization or individual under a contractual agreement? . . . . ☐ Yes   X No

b   Is the organization a party to any leases? . . . . ☐ Yes   X No

If either of these questions is answered "Yes," attach a copy of each such contract and explain the relationship between the applicant and each of the other parties.

The program is run by are employees who are employed by the Board of Directors.

10   Is the organization a membership organization? . . . . ☐ Yes   X No
If "Yes," complete the following:

a   Describe the organization's membership requirements and attach a schedule of membership fees and dues.

b   Describe your present and proposed efforts to attract members and attach a copy of any descriptive literature or promotional material used for this purpose.

c   What benefits do (or will) your members receive in exchange for their payment of dues?

11a   If the organization provides benefits, services or products, are the recipients required, or will they be required, to pay for them? . . . . ☐ N/A   X Yes   ☐ No
If "Yes," explain; show how the charges are determined; and attach a copy of your current fee schedule.

Parents are assessed for registration, enrollment and monthly tuition fees according the attached tuition fee schedule.
Parents are assessed for registration, enrollment and monthly tuition fees according the attached tuition fee schedule.

b   Does or will the organization limit its benefits, services or products to specific individuals or classes of individuals? . . . . ☐ N/A   X Yes   ☐ No
If "Yes," explain how the recipients or beneficiaries are or will be selected.

School-age children in kindergarten through 6th grade.

12   Does or will the organization attempt to influence legislation? . . . . ☐ Yes   X No
If "Yes," explain. Also, give an estimate of the percentage of the organization's time and funds which it devotes or plans to devote to this activity.

13   Does or will the organization intervene in any way in political campaigns, including the publication or distribution of statements? . . . . ☐ Yes   X No
If "Yes," explain fully.

Part III. Technical Requirements

1.   WBASP is filing Form 1023 within 15 months of the date (stamped by the Secretary of State) on the articles of incorporation which were filed with the Secretary of State.

Part III Technical Requirements

1 Are you filing Form 1023 within 15 months from the end of the month in which you were created or formed? X **Yes** ☐ **No**
If you answer "Yes," do not answer questions 2 through 6.

2 If one of the exceptions to the 15-month filing requirement shown below applies, check the appropriate box and proceed to question 7.

Exceptions—You are not required to file an exemption application within 15 months if the organization:

☐ **(a)** Is a church, interchurch organization, local unit of a church, a convention or association of churches, or an integrated auxiliary of a church;

☐ **(b)** Is not a private foundation and normally has gross receipts of not more than $5,000 in each tax year; or,

☐ **(c)** Is a subordinate organization covered by a group exemption letter, but only if the parent or supervisory organization timely submitted a notice covering the subordinate.

3 If you do not meet any of the exceptions in question 2, do you wish to request relief from the 15-month filing requirement? . . . . ☐ **Yes** ☐ **No**

4 If you answer "Yes" to question 3, please give your reasons for not filing this application within 15 months from the end of the month in which your organization was created or formed.

5 If you answer "No" to both questions 1 and 3 and do not meet any of the exceptions in question 2, your qualification as a section 501(c)(3) organization can be recognized only from the date this application is filed with your key District Director. Therefore, do you want us to consider your application as a request for recognition of exemption as a section 501(c)(3) organization from the date the application is received and not retroactively to the date you were formed? . . . . ☐ **Yes** ☐ **No**

6 If you answer "Yes" to question 5 above and wish to request recognition of section 501(c)(4) status for the period beginning with the date you were formed and ending with the date your Form 1023 application was received (the effective date of your section 501(c)(3) status), check here ► ☐ and attach a completed page 1 of Form 1024 to this application.

7. WBASP is not a private foundation (No).

8. WBASP is not a private operating foundation (No).

9. WBASP has indicated (i) since it qualifies under Section 509 (a)(2).

Part III Technical Requirements *(Continued)*

7 Is the organization a private foundation?
   ☐ **Yes** (Answer question 8.)
   X **No** (Answer question 9 and proceed as instructed.)

8 If you answer "Yes" to question 7, do you claim to be a private operating foundation?
   ☐ **Yes** (Complete Schedule E)
   ☐ **No**

   After answering this question, go to Part IV.

9 If you answer "No" to question 7, indicate the public charity classification you are requesting by checking the box below that most appropriately applies:

THE ORGANIZATION IS NOT A PRIVATE FOUNDATION BECAUSE IT QUALIFIES:

(a)	☐ As a church or a convention or association of churches (MUST COMPLETE SCHEDULE A.)	Sections 509(a)(1) and 170(b)(1)(A)(i)
(b)	☐ As a school (MUST COMPLETE SCHEDULE B).	Sections 509(a)(1) and 170(b)(1)(A)(ii)
(c)	☐ As a hospital or a cooperative hospital service organization, or a medical research organization operated in conjunction with a hospital (MUST COMPLETE SCHEDULE C).	Sections 509(a)(1) and 170(b)(1)(A)(iii)
(d)	☐ As a governmental unit described in section 170(c)(1).	Sections 509(a)(1) and 170(b)(1)(A)(v)
(e)	☐ As being operated solely for the benefit of, or in connection with, one or more of the organizations described in (a) through (d), (g), (h), or (i) (MUST COMPLETE SCHEDULE D).	Section 509(a)(3)
(f)	☐ As being organized and operated exclusively for testing for public safety.	Section 509(a)(4)
(g)	☐ As being operated for the benefit of a college or university that is owned or operated by a governmental unit.	Sections 509(a)(1) and 170(b)(1)(A)(iv)
(h)	☐ As receiving a substantial part of its support in the form of contributions from publicly supported organizations, from a governmental unit, or from the general public.	Sections 509(a)(1) and 170(b)(1)(A)(vi)
(i)	X As normally receiving not more than one-third of its support from gross investment income and more than one-third of its support from contributions, membership fees, and gross receipts from activities related to its exempt functions (subject to certain exceptions).	Section 509(a)(2)
(j)	☐ We are a publicly supported organization but are not sure whether we meet the public support test of block (h) or block (i). We would like the Internal Revenue Service to decide the proper classification.	Sections 509(a)(1) and 170(b)(1)(A)(vi) or Section 509(a)(2)

**If you checked one of the boxes (a) through (f) in question 9, go to question 14.
If you checked box (g) in question 9, go to questions 11 and 12.
If you checked box (h), (i), or (j), go to question 10.**

10. WBASP has completed a tax year of 12 months and requests a definitive ruling.

11. WBASP has indicated one unusual grant given by the state Department of Human Services for start-up expenses.

12. Non-applicable.

13a. WBASP has no disqualified persons.
13b. WBASP has received no line 9 payment more than $5,000.00.

14. WBASP has indicated that it will complete Schedule G.

Part III **Technical Requirements** *(Continued)*

10 If you checked box (h), (i), or (j) in question 9, have you completed a tax year of at least 8 months?

☐ No—You must request an advance ruling by completing and signing 2 Forms 872-C and attaching them to your application.

X Yes—Indicate whether you are requesting:

 X A definitive ruling (Answer question 11 through and including question 14.)

 ☐ An advance ruling (Answer questions 11 and 14 and attach 2 Forms 872-C completed and signed.)

11 If the organization received any unusual grants during any of the tax years shown in Part IV-A, attach a list for each year showing the name of the contributor; the date and the amount of the grant; and a brief description of the nature of each such grant.

See Child Day Care Start-Up Grant from Iowa Dept. of Human Services attachment. This was a one-time, non-renewable grant program.

12 If you are requesting a definitive ruling under section 170(b)(1)(A)(iv) or (vi), check here ▶ ☐ and:

 a Enter 2% of line 8, column (e) of Part IV-A _____

 b Attach a list showing the name and amount contributed by each person (other than a governmental unit or "publicly supported" organization) whose total gifts, grants, contributions, etc., were more than the amount you entered on line **12a** above.

13 If you are requesting a definitive ruling under section 509(a)(2), check here ▶ **X** and:

 a For each of the years included on lines 1, 2, and 9 of Part IV-A, attach a list showing the name of and amount received from each person who is a "disqualified person." **We have no disqualified persons.**

 b For each of the years included on line 9 of Part IV-A, attach a list showing the name of and amount received from each payer (other than a "disqualified person") whose payments to the organization were more than $5,000. For this purpose, "payer" includes, but is not limited to, any organization described in sections 170(b)(1)(A)(i) through (vi) and any governmental agency or bureau.

14 Indicate if your organization is one of the following, and if so, complete the required schedule. (Submit only those schedules, if any, that apply to your organization. **Do not submit blank schedules.**)

	Yes	No	If "Yes," complete schedule:
Is the organization a church?			A
Is the organization, or any part of it, a school?			B
Is the organization, or any part of it, a hospital or medical research organization?			C
Is the organization a section 509(a)(3) supporting organization?			D
Is the organization an operating foundation?			E
Is the organization, or any part of it, a home for the aged or handicapped?			F
Is the organization, or any part of it, a child care organization?		X	G
Does the organization provide or administer any scholarship benefits, student aid, etc.?			H
Has the organization taken over, or will it take over, the facilities of a "for profit" institution?			I

13. b. Please see attachment re Child Day Care Start-Up Grant from Iowa Dept. of Human Services in the amount of **$5,000.00**

Part IV. Financial Data

A. WBASP has displayed the revenue (income) figures from its current tax year. It has indicated income on lines 9 and 10, the unusual grant on line 12, and the income total on line 13.

WBASP has displayed the expenses figures from its current tax year. Staff salaries are indicated on line 18 and all other expenses are shown on line 22. The income and expenses spreadsheet attachment serves as the requested schedule. Total expenses are indicated on line 23 and the balance of revenue against expenses is shown on line 24.

Part IV Financial Data

Complete the financial statements for the current year and for each of the 3 years immediately before it. If in existence less than 4 years, complete the statements for each year in existence. **If in existence less than 1 year, also provide proposed budgets for the 2 years following the current year.**

A.—Statement of Revenue and Expenses

		Current tax year (a) From 6/30/89 to 6/30/90	(b) 19 6/30/91	(c) 19 6/30/92	(d) 19	(e) TOTAL
Revenue	1 Gifts, grants, and contributions received (not including unusual grants—see instructions)					
	2 Membership fees received					
	3 Gross investment income (see instructions for definition)					
	4 Net income from organization's unrelated business activities not included on line 3					
	5 Tax revenues levied for and either paid to or spent on behalf of the organization					
	6 Value of services or facilities furnished by a governmental unit to the organization without charge (not including the value of services or facilities generally furnished the public without charge)					
	7 Other income (not including gain or loss from sale of capital assets) (attach schedule)					
	8 **Total** of lines 1 through 7					
	9 Gross receipts from admissions, sales of merchandise or services, or furnishing of facilities in any activity that is not an unrelated business within the meaning of section 513	$32,300.00	$30,440.00	$35,480.00		$98,220.00
	10 **Total** of lines 8 and 9	$32,300.00	$30,440.00	$35,480.00		$98,220.00
	11 Gain or loss from sale of capital assets (attach schedule)					
	12 Unusual grants	$5.000.00				$5,000.00
	13 **Total** revenue (add lines 10 through 12)	$37,300.00	$30,440.00	$35,480.00		$103,220.00
Expenses	14 Fundraising expenses					
	15 Contributions, gifts, grants, and similar amounts paid (attach schedule)					
	16 Disbursements to or for benefit of members (attach schedule)					
	17 Compensation of officers, directors, and trustees (attach schedule)					
	18 Other salaries and wages	$23,318.10	$24,250.82	$25,220.86		
	19 Interest					
	20 Occupancy (rent, utilities, etc.)					
	21 Depreciation and depletion					
	22 Other (attach schedule)	$6,705.00	$5,539.80	$5,856.86		
	23 **Total** expenses	$30,023.10	$29,790.62	$31,077.72		
	24 Excess of revenue over expenses (line 13 minus line 23)	$7,276.90	$649.38	$4,402.28		

B.

1. WBASP has shown its cash on hand.

2. WBASP has attached displayed the replacement cost of its supplies and equipment on hand. An inventory of these items should be attached.

11. WBASP has indicated its total assets.

16. WBASP has no liabilities.

17. WBASP has displayed its total fund balances and net assets.

18. WBASP has displayed its net worth.

Part IV   **Financial Data** *(Continued)*

			Current tax year
B.—Balance Sheet (at the end of the period shown)			Date 6/30/90

Assets

1	Cash Balance will be used to fund fall start up.	1	$7,276.90
2	Accounts receivable, net	2	
3	Inventories	3	
4	Bonds and notes receivable (attach schedule)	4	
5	Corporate stocks (attach schedule)	5	
6	Mortgage loans (attach schedule)	6	
7	Other investments (attach schedule)	7	
8	Depreciable and depletable assets (attach schedule) Used toys and games	8	$978.22
9	Land	9	
10	Other assets (attach schedule)	10	
11	**Total assets**	11	$8,255.12

Liabilities

12	Accounts payable	12	
13	Contributions, gifts, grants, etc., payable	13	
14	Mortgages and notes payable (attach schedule)	14	
15	Other liabilities (attach schedule)	15	
16	**Total liabilities**	16	$0.00

Fund Balances or Net Assets

17	Total fund balances or net assets	17	$8,255.12
18	**Total liabilities and fund balances or net assets** (add line 16 and line 17)	18	$8,255.12

If there has been any substantial change in any aspect of your financial activities since the end of the period shown above, check the box and attach a detailed explanation . . . . ▶ ☐

Schedule G. - Child Care Organizations

1. WBASP answers Yes, its primary function is to provide care for children away from home.

2. WBASP is licensed by the DHS to serve no more than 30 children at a time. Average attendance at each session has been 28.

3. 36 children are enrolled in WBASP during various sessions of the week.

4. All of the parents of WBASP children are gainfully employed or while their children are cared for by the program.

5. WBASP's services are available to any child in K-6th grades.

6. WBASP's services are available to working parents, or parents looking for work, as well as anyone with the ability to pay.

7. WBASP does not operate a school (No).

Schedule G.—Child Care Organizations

1 Is the organization's primary activity the providing of care for children away
from their homes? . . . . X **Yes**   ☐ **No**

2 How many children is the organization authorized to care for by the state (or local governmental
unit) and what was the average attendance during the past 6 months, or the number of months the
organization has been in existence if less than 6 months?

The program is licensed for no more than 30 children to be cared for at a time. Average attendance has been 30.

3 How many children are currently cared for by the organization?

4 Is substantially all (at least 85%) of the care provided for the purpose of
enabling parent(s) to be gainfully employed or to seek employment? . . . . . . X **Yes**   ☐ **No**

5 Are the services provided available to the general public? . . . . X **Yes**   ☐ **No**
If "No," explain.

6 Indicate the category, or categories, of parents whose children are eligible for your child-care
services (check as many as apply):

☐   low income parents

X   any working parents (or parents looking for work)

X   anyone with the ability to pay

☐   other (explain)

7 Do you operate a school? . . . . ☐ **Yes**   X **No**
If "Yes," complete Schedule B.

Instructions

Line 5.— If your services are not available to the general public, indicate the particular group or groups
that may utilize your services.

Line 7.— Providing for the care of children away from their homes is an exempt purpose (educational)
as described in section 501(c)(3) of the Internal Revenue Code. However, a child care
organization is not a school unless it: (1) has the primary function of presenting formal
instruction; (2) normally maintains a regular faculty and curriculum; (3) normally has a
regular enrolled body of students; and (4) has a place where educational activities are
carried on.

D

BEFORE AND AFTER SCHOOL PROGRAM

POLICIES AND PROCEDURES

PARENT HANDBOOK

INTRODUCTION

Welcome to the Before and After School Program. Our child care program has been organized to provide supervision for children in kindergarten through sixth grade. The Program is a state licensed, non-profit corporation, administered by a parent board and child care director. The Parent Handbook is a valid part of the enrollment agreement between the Before and After School Program and the parents or guardians of children who are enrolled in the Program.

GOALS

The Program will provide quality child care which parents can rely upon throughout the school calendar year, as defined by the River City Community School District calendar.

The Program will offer a variety of activities which includes recreation and games, arts and crafts, reading, music, time to work on homework, and "free time" for the children to pursue their own interests in a safe, friendly environment.

TABLE OF POLICIES AND PROCEDURES

POLICIES & PROCEDURES

ENROLLMENT IN THE BEFORE & AFTER SCHOOL PROGRAM CONSTITUTES AN UNDERSTANDING THAT YOU WILL ABIDE BY THE POLICIES LISTED AS FOLLOWS:

SECTION I. PARENT'S EXPECTATIONS OF THE PROGRAM

Parents may expect that:

1. Their children are cared for in a safe, supportive environment.
2. They may visit with the Director about concerns related to their child or the program.
3. They will be told about any misbehavior on the part of their child, and to visit with the Child Care Director in order to bring about improvement in the situation.
4. They will be informed promptly if their child does not arrive at the Program according to his/her enrollment information.
5. They will be regularly informed by the Child Care Director about Program activities.

SECTION II. PROGRAM'S EXPECTATIONS OF THE PARENTS

The Program expects that parents will:

1. Pay fees on time as explained in Section V. Fees and Payment Policy.
2. Keep the child's records up-to-date as explained in Section VIII. Enrollment Forms.
3. Pick up children on time as explained in Section XI. Afternoon Closing Time.
4. Follow health policy as explained in Section XVI. Health Policy.
5. Contact the Director if their child will not be attending on a scheduled day.
6. Pay attention to any communications from the Director regarding their child's behavior, and cooperate in efforts to bring about improvement in the situation.

SECTION III. CHILDREN'S EXPECTATIONS OF THE PROGRAM

Children may expect:

1. To have a safe, supportive and consistent environment.
2. To use all the program equipment, materials and facilities on an equal basis.
3. To receive respectful treatment.
4. To have discipline that is fair and non-punitive.
5. To receive nurturing care from staff members who are actively involved with them.

SECTION IV. PROGRAM'S EXPECTATIONS OF THE CHILDREN

The Program expects that the children will:

1. Be responsible for their actions.
2. Respect the school rules that guide them during the day and while at the Program.
3. Remain with the group and child care staff at all times.
4. Take care of materials and equipment properly and return them to their place when done, or before taking out new ones.
5. Arrive at the Program promptly, according to the enrollment information.

SECTION V. FEES AND PAYMENT POLICY

The Program salaries, supplies and administrative expenses are supported entirely by fees. The River City Community School District provides the space, utilities and custodial services as an in-kind donation to the Program. Fees are as follows:

A. BEFORE SCHOOL: $21.00 per month
B. AFTER SCHOOL: $84.00 per month
C. COMBINED: $105.00 per month

1. Registration and enrollment fees are non-refundable.

2. Tuition payments are due the first school day of each month and are paid to reserve an entire month of child care, according to the option agreement, irrespective of the actual number of days and/hours the child attends.

3. Any tuition that is not paid by the last day of the first full week of the month in which it is due will result in an immediate suspension of child care services until the fees are paid in full. If the tuition is not paid in full by the end of the second full week the child shall be automatically discharged from the Program. Reinstatement may occur on a space-available basis when all fees have been paid.

4. Non-sufficient fund checks are held until a cash or money order is received by the Program to cover the amount of the check. Parents will pay a $10.00 charge for a NSF check. Parents will be notified immediately upon receipt of the NSF notice by the program and shall have two school days in which to pay the charge and tuition in full by cash or equivalent. If not paid by the end of the second day after notice, child care services will be suspended immediately. If the tuition and charge is not paid in full by the end of the first full week after notice, the child will be discharged from the program.

5. If a child withdraws or is discharged from the Program, tuition will be due for the balance of the month or for one-half month, which ever amount is greater.

6. If all of the child's required enrollment forms are not completed and returned to the Child Care Director by the day the child is scheduled to start the Program, the child will not be allowed to attend until these completed forms are submitted to the Child Care Director. The parent/guardian/ custodian will be responsible for payment of monthly fees from starting from that date in order to reserve the enrollment spot until such time as the completed forms are returned.

SECTION VI. IRS STATEMENTS

The Program does not provide an itemized statement for tax purposes. We suggest that you keep a record of your monthly checks as an accurate account of your child care expenses. We will provide you with our taxpayer identification number for the Child Care Expenses form.

SECTION VII. REGISTRATION AND ENROLLMENT

The Program encourages children of all backgrounds to attend. The Program does not discriminate on the basis of sex, race, color, creed, national origin or ethnic background.

Registration: The parent must complete a registration form and submit it with a $20.00 non-refundable registration fee to the Child Care Director. Registered children who cannot be immediately enrolled, will be placed on a waiting list.

Eligibility: A child may be registered for enrollment in the program at any time. Children must be in grades K-6 to be eligible for enrollment.

Openings: Full and part-time openings are determined on the basis of FTEs (full time equivalents) and the number of FTEs permitted by the program's license. When full or part-time child care openings occur, parents of registered children are contacted for enrollment on the basis of: 1) the schedule indicated on the registration form, and, 2) on a first-come basis for the available time according to the date of registration receipt.

Enrollment: Parents of registered children will be contacted regarding enrollment in the program.

1. If the parents wish to enroll their child(ren), the parents will be provided with a set(s) of enrollment forms. Prior to the child's first to the first day of attendance, the parent(s) will complete all forms and submit them to the Child Care Director. A completed set of forms is required for each child enrolled in the program.

2. Upon enrollment, the parent must make payment to the Child Care Director of a non-refundable enrollment fee and first month tuition fee. The parent must sign and return a program registration agreement.

3. Children will be allowed to attend the program only after all forms have been completed and returned, and payments have been submitted. If the parent has not submitted completed forms after the date when the child was scheduled to start attendance, the parent will be responsible for payment of monthly fees in order to reserve the enrollment spot until such time as the completed forms are returned.

SECTION VIII. ENROLLMENT FORMS

Parents will be asked to complete the following:

Enrollment Form	**Release Form**	**Physical Assessment**
Record of Immunizations	**Emergency Medical Consent**	**Arrival/Departure Forms**
Medication Release (as needed)		

The Program expects the forms to be kept current. The parent must provide new information to the director regarding information on forms such as: emergency persons, names, employers, phone numbers, arrival/departure changes.

SECTION IX. WITHDRAWAL FROM THE PROGRAM

Parents wishing to withdraw their child from the Program must provide a statement in writing at least 30 days prior to the discontinuation of this service. Tuition will be due for the balance of the month or for one-half month, which ever amount is greater.

SECTION X. HOURS OF OPERATION

Morning Program: 7:00 AM to 8:30 AM: Weather conditions can make it difficult for caregivers and custodians to get to school on schedule. For your child's safety, please make sure that the school doors are unlocked and that the caregivers are on duty before leaving your child at school.

Afternoon Program: 3:00 PM to 6:00 PM

SECTION XI. AFTERNOON CLOSING TIME

The Program closes at 6:00 PM. Parents whose children remain past 6:00 PM must pay overtime fees as follows:

5 - 15 minutes overtime - $5.00 per child

Each additional 1-15 minutes, $5.00 per child

Late fees are paid directly to the caregiver who must stay late.

Child care services may be withdrawn if three overtime charges occur.

SECTION XII. ABSENCES

If your child will not be attending the Program because of scheduled appointment, vacations, or other planned absences, please notify the Child Care Director in advance. If your child is ill, when you call the school to report the illness or pick up your child from school, please request the school secretary to put a notice of the child's absence in the Program mailbox. Absentees without prior notification may be mistaken for a missing child and unnecessary concern and time spent in searching for the child may occur. If a child does not arrive at the program as intended, the Child Care Director will contact the parents. If the parents cannot be reached, the Director will contact the child's emergency persons.

SECTION XIII. RELEASE OF CHILDREN

Children will arrive at and leave the Program according to the schedule written by parents on the Arrival/Departure Procedures Form. Children will be allowed to leave with persons other than the parent only if permission has been given to the director on the enrollment form or in writing by the parent. If a one-time exception is made to this schedule, the parents should provide the Child Care Director with a completed Exception to Arrival/Departure Procedures Form prior to the date.

If your child attends extracurricular activities or has any other kind of arrival/departure time change within the period he/she is enrolled in the Program, you must provide the Child Care Director with a completed a Change of Arrival/Departure Procedures Form, prior to the date the change is effective.

SECTION XIV. SCHEDULED & UNSCHEDULED NO-SCHOOL, SCHOOL OPENING DELAYS AND SCHOOL CLOSINGS

1. **Scheduled No-School Days** - The Board will notify parents in advance whether the Program will be available on scheduled no-school days such as conference days.
2. **Unscheduled No-School Days** - There will be no Program on days when school is canceled due to water main breaks, heating failure, electrical problems, weather, etc.
3. **Unscheduled School Delays** - The Program will not be open in the morning if school is delayed due to water main breaks, heating failure, electrical problems, weather, etc.
4. **Scheduled Early Dismissal Days** - The Board will notify parents in advance whether services will be available on scheduled early dismissal days.
5. **Unscheduled Early Dismissal Days** - The Program is not available when school is dismissed early due to water, heating, electrical problems, weather, etc.

SECTION XV. DISTRIBUTION OF MEDICATIONS

Whenever a child is to be given prescription or over-the-counter medicine, the parent must provide the program director a completed, signed medication authorization form to the director. The medication must be provided in the original or duplicate container, or a container accompanied by the doctor's directions.

If medication is to be kept at the Program for treatment of a chronic condition, no more than a one month supply should remain at the Program at any time.

SECTION XVI. HEALTH AND SAFETY POLICY

If your child has a known medical condition (asthma, diabetes, seizure disorder, etc.) please be sure the director knows what to do if a problem should occur during Program hours. Please make sure that any medication is available and that the appropriate forms for its use have been completed.

If a child has any one of the following conditions, the parent will be notified to pick up the child immediately: **Contagious Disease, Fever over 100 F, Vomiting or Diarrhea, Accident Requiring Medical Attention.**

In case of accident or illness, parents of the child will be called immediately. In serious cases, the child will be taken to one of the local hospitals by emergency vehicle for treatment and the parents will be called as soon as possible.

Outdoor play will not be allowed when temperature (including wind chill) falls below 0 degrees.

In the case of someone appearing on the premises with a firearm, the emergency number (911) should be called and children should be taken out of danger and given aid.

Caregivers are to make every effort to keep a child from getting into a car with a parent under the influence of drugs or alcohol. They should call the police to give the child and parent a ride home. Caregivers should not under any circumstances give transportation to a parent who appears to be impaired by drugs or alcohol because the Program insurance does not cover transportation related to the Program.

The Program's license requires caregivers to report suspected cases of child abuse. This includes the reporting of parents who appear to be impaired by drugs or alcohol.

SECTION XVII. INSURANCE

The Program carries minimal liability insurance, but has no financial resources of its own. Families are encouraged to provide their own insurance coverage. Many families are covered by the parent's policy at work, and/or their own private policies. Public school students may sign up for accident insurance in the fall of each year. Parents who wish to enroll should check with the school office.

SECTION XVIII. BREAKFAST AND SNACK

Morning Program - We serve a nutritious breakfast at 7:45 a.m.

Afternoon Program - We serve nutritious snacks in the afternoon Program. Parents may want to provide a treat in honor of a child's birthday. In this case, they should contact the director to determine the number of children to be served and plan the date.

SECTION XIX. CHILD'S PERSONAL PROPERTY

Children's personal property, coats, clothing, school bags, etc. must be cleared from the child care room after each session of the program. Any personal property which remains after the session will be taken to the school office lost and found box. Although the Program attempts to help children stay organized, the Program cannot be responsible for lost personal property.

Children should not bring money, toys, food or other items not necessary for school activities to the program without checking with the director.

SECTION XX. VISITORS AND OBSERVATIONS

Parents and community members who are screened by the director are welcome to observe at the Program. For liability and supervision reasons it is not possible for children who visit the program to take part in activities.

SECTION XXII. DISCIPLINE AND DISCHARGE

Children are entitled to a pleasant and harmonious environment at the Program. The Before and After School Program cannct serve children whose display chronically disruptive behavior.

Chronically disruptive behavior is defined as verbal or physical activity which may include but is not limited to such behavior that: requires constant attention from the staff, inflicts physical or emotional harm on other children, abuses the staff, ignores or disobeys the rules which guide behavior during the school day and Program time. If a child cannot adjust to the Program setting and behave appropriately, then the child may be discharged.

Reasonable efforts will be made to assist children to adjust to the Program setting. Disruptive behavior will be dealt with in the following manner:

1.   The misbehaving child will be given a five minute time-out, in order for him/her to cool off and think about his/her actions.

2.   If a second, 10 minute time-out is given to the child in a single day, an incident report will be written by the caregiver. This report is to be given to the parent or guardian to read and sign. The report will be returned to the caregiver where it will remain with the child's enrollment information.

3.   If a child receives three written behavior-related incident reports, the child will be suspended effective at the end of the day of the third report. During the first week of the suspension, the parents, caregiver and a member of the Board of Directors, other than the child's parent, will meet in a conference setting in order to determine the conditions for reinstatement. **Parents will be responsible for the payment of tuition during the period of suspension or until the child is withdrawn from the Program or is discharged by action of the Board of Directors. Tuition and refund policies shall be as set out in Section V. Fees and Payment, #3 and #4.**

4.   If the child is reinstated in the program and receives a fourth behavior-related incident report, the director may suspend the child immediately, including if necessary, notifying the parent to come and get the child. The director may make such recommendations to the Board of Directors as are appropriate, including discharge without the right of reinstatement. The director will bring this to the prompt attention of the Board of Directors who will act upon the recommendations of the director regarding continuation of the child in the program. **Parents will continue to be responsible for the payment of tuition during the period of suspension or until the child is withdrawn from the Program or is discharged by action of the Board of Directors, who will notify the parent. Tuition and refund policies shall be as set out in Section V. Fees and Payment, #3 and #4.**

5.   If the severity of a problem is great enough that it could endanger the safety of the child or other children in the Program, discharge will be effective immediately after the director consults with the Board of Directors who will notify the parent.

A child may be discharged if he/she is picked up late three times. (See Section XI. Afternoon Closing Time).

A child may be discharged for non-payment of fees as discussed in Section V. Fees and Payment, #3 and #4.

BEFORE AND AFTER SCHOOL PROGRAM

BOARD MANUAL

THE BOARD MANUAL

Well planned board manuals are intended to serve each member of a volunteer board from his or her orientation through the term of service. Manuals are intended to be frequently consulted and updated. They are the basic tool of the responsible board member. Use of the board manual promotes more orderly, effective program operation.

New and Replacement Pages
This board manual will be passed on to your replacement at the end of your term of service. Since volunteer boards turn over periodically, it is crucial that new members are provided with complete and accurate program information. For program continuity it is very important that new and replacement pages be added.

Annual Review
The board manual should be reviewed annually to insure that its contents reflect current practices. Changes in the contents of the board manual should be acted upon by the Board.

Manual Contents
The Before and After School Program is governed by the statements set forth in the Articles of Incorporation, Bylaws, Staff Handbook and Parent Handbook. It is absolutely vital that information contained in these documents be kept current.

Lined notebook paper may be inserted into the board manual in a section called "Notes." This enables board members to keep all of their BASP materials together.

Manual sections should include:

Master Calendar	**Board Information**
Program Directory	**Minutes**
Budget	**Space & Equipment Agreement**
Parent Handbook	**Staff Handbook**
Articles/Bylaws	**Forms**
Licensing	**Notes**

TOPICAL MEETING CALENDAR

The Before and After School Program Board of Directors is required to meet quarterly, and probably will meet more frequently. All meetings of the Board are open to the membership. The place, date and time of board meetings should be announced in writing and posted in a conspicuous location at the Program at least a week prior to the meeting. The Board will also convene at least one, and probably two general members meetings each year. After Board meetings, minutes will be promptly transcribed and posted at the Program. The Board may, at its discretion, go into executive session in the event of confidential matters. If this occurs, it will be noted in the meeting minutes.

The Board of Directors may employ a topical meeting calendar to guide their business and programmatic activities. A model topical calendar follows:

August
Review the number of enrollments
Receive report on paper compliance of enrollments and staff
Perform self-study regarding conformance with licensing regulations
Receive report on annual September start up and operating budget
Assign staff evaluation and staff probationary evaluation tasks
Goal-setting for the year

September
Parent Orientation Meeting

October
Review comments and actions taken related to licensing inspection
Review plan for staff development to take place during year
Review and adjust staff/parent policies and procedures as needed
Receive and review staff probationary evaluations
Review status of budget and tuition fees, adjust as needed

January
Announce and initiate search for new board members
Conduct review of parent/staff handbooks, forms and contracts
Receive and review report regarding staff evaluation
Review staff salaries; consider adjustments
Commence planning for next year's operating budget
Arrange for next school-year's insurance
Make arrangements for annual IRS filings
Report on progress toward goals set in September

March
Commence registration process
Commence recruitment to fill staff openings
Commence preparation of the annual report

April
General Members Meeting
Annual Report and Elections

May
Offer contracts
Finalize and approve next school year's start-up and operating budget

BOARD OPERATIONS

Volunteer leadership today in non-profit child care organizations has never been greater. Board members are accountable for a wide array of activities often far removed from their professional training.

They are expected to develop long-range plans both for funding as well as programming; they are expected to stay current with licensing regulations and legislative issues affecting child care; they are expected to know and employ budgeting techniques; they are expected to motivate their staff to peak performance; all aimed at insuring that the child care services being delivered meet their goal that the children be cared for in a safe, happy environment.

In short, child care boards are small business operators. Their overall objective is to provide child care services to families in an effective and efficient mode.

AREAS OF PROGRAM OPERATIONS

Below are listed some of the responsibilities of the Board of Directors and Child Care Director. There is some duplication between the Board and Child Care Director. This is not surprising, since the Board delegates some of the responsibilities to the Child Care Director.

<u>General Administration</u>:
The day-to-day functioning of the Program including:
     Supervision of staff
     Activity Program
     Maintenance of facilities
     Daily record keeping
     Public relations
     Legal activity
     Policy formulation and implementation
     Contacting state and local regulatory agencies
     Scheduling the use of facilities
     Determining enrollment policies
     Conforming to health, safety and licensing regulations

<u>Board Relations</u>:
A key function of the Board which includes:
     Board Meetings
     Formal and Informal Communications Between Meetings

Financial Management:
General fiscal accountability both externally and internally which includes:
>Development of budgets
>Operating within the budget
>Fund raising
>Grant writing and administration
>Payroll
>Bookkeeping and Auditing
>Tax information, records and filings
>Inventory of program equipment
>Collecting fees and tuition
>Preparing monthly financial reports on the status of the budget

Personnel:
Concerned with all the functions regarding staff:
>Preparation of Job Descriptions
>Recruitment and Selection
>Staff Development
>Wage and Salary Determination
>Termination of Staff
>Evaluation of Staff
>Determination of Terms of Employment
>Preparation of an Annual Staff Handbook
>Preparation of Staff Contracts
>Keeping Personnel Records

Program Development:
Although some people may differ as to the amount of involvement on the part of the Board in the development of programs, this is fundamentally a responsibility shared by both the Board and Child Care Director:
>Evaluation of the Group of Children Served
>Determination of Needs of Children Being Served
>Development of Programming Suited to Needs
>Periodic Evaluation of Programming
>Planning for Program Enrichment

Community Relations:
A key function of the Board and Child Care Director which has a positive impact on the public confidence in the Program and aids in the enrollment of children:

> Regular Communication with the School Administration
> Communication with the Public via School Newsletter,
> Media, Marketing Pamphlets, etc.
> Communication with other BASPs
> Orientation of Parents
> Preparation of an annual Parent Handbook

VOLUNTEER BOARD MEMBERS

Persons who agree to serve on a volunteer board understand that this is a serious commitment. A good board member is dedicated to helping others through the administration of a safe, happy child care program. He or she approaches this commitment in a manner which includes:

1. **Treating staff and other board members as partners**
2. **Reliable performance of tasks**
3. **Dependable, prepared meeting attendance**
4. **Criticizes, when necessary, in a constructive way**
5. **Keeps disagreements impersonal; tries to promote unity**
6. **Welcomes information and advice, but makes own decisions**
7. **Accepts that decisions must be made by the majority vote**
8. **Respects the right of others to disagree with him or her and to have a fair hearing of their points of view**
9. **Maintains loyalty to the Program and its goals**

BOARD MEETINGS

Board meetings are the focal point of Board communication and decision-making. Board members should expect an agenda prior to the meeting and minutes after each meeting.

The Board of Directors is required to meet quarterly, and probably will meet with somewhat more frequency. All meetings of the Board are open to the membership. The place, date and time of board meetings should be announced in writing and posted in a conspicuous location at the Program at least a week prior to the meeting. After Board meetings, minutes will be promptly transcribed and posted at the Program.

The Board may, at its discretion, go into executive session in the event of confidential matters. If this occurs, it will be noted in the meeting minutes.

Meetings should be planned according to the needs of the agenda. Since long evening meetings are problematic, and meeting frequency can be an issue with volunteers who have limited amounts of available time, the Chair must consider the type of agenda items when calling a meeting. When an agenda item calls for much discussion, such as evaluation, or policy-making, the number of items on the agenda needs to be brief. When the agenda consists mainly of reports and items easily covered, the list may be longer. The purposes of Board meetings include:

1. **To hear reports from the Child Care Director and Chair**
2. **To make policy decisions**
3. **To advise**
4. **To legitimatize**
5. **To communicate**
6. **To organize**
7. **To plan**
8. **To hear treasurer's report**
9. **To meet legal requirements for Board meetings.**

BOARD AND CHILD CARE DIRECTOR RELATIONSHIP

While the backbone of a child care program is the volunteer Board, a successful child care program must have a good Child Care Director. Excellent programs demonstrate a solid working relationship between the two parties. This relationship is more solidified when both parties understand their roles and responsibilities. The Child Care Director should be able to expect that a Board will:

1. **Counsel and advise, giving the benefit of its judgement and familiarity with the local setting.**
2. **Consult with the Child Care Director on all matters which the Board is considering.**
3. **Share all communications with the Child Care Director.**
4. **Provide support to the Child Care Director in carrying out professional duties.**
5. **Support the Child Care Director in all decisions and actions consistent with policies of the Board and the licensing standards.**
6. **Evaluate the work of the Child Care Director.**
7. **Act according to the terms of employment set forth in the staff handbook and the employee's contract.**
8. **Receive and review the board reports submitted by the Child Care Director.**

CHILD CARE DIRECTOR'S BOARD REPORT

This report covers the period from _____ to _____ .

Highlights of the Activity Program (themes, projects, movies, special guests):

_____
_____
_____
_____
_____

Administrative Activities of the Child Care Director:

_____
_____
_____

Information related to Staff:

_____
_____
_____

Areas of Difficulty:

_____
_____
_____

Financial Needs or Considerations of the Program:

_____
_____
_____

Proposals/Requests for Board Action:

_____
_____
_____

_____   _____

Date   Child Care Director

MANUAL INDEX TABS

These fit into the 8 page index tab pages which can be purchased inexpensively as sets. Duplicate one page per manual and place into plastic index tab holders.

Calendars	Board
Minutes	Budget
Directory	Art/Bylaws
Parent Hbk	Staff Hbk
Agreement	Forms
Licensing	Notes

F

BEFORE AND AFTER SCHOOL PROGRAM

STAFF RECRUITMENT AND EMPLOYMENT

MODEL PROCEDURES AND FORMS

STAFFING SCHOOL-AGE CHILD CARE PROGRAMS

Staff performance ultimately determines the success of any child care program. Boards must define staff job descriptions, and utilize effective procedures for determining the qualifications which will be required of candidates for those positions. These activities are among the most important tasks undertaken by a child care board of directors. An outline of the process and terms of employment may be found in the 200 section of the Staff Handbook (Section G), and related forms in the Form Book (Section I), of this manual.

STAFF QUALIFICATIONS

State Departments of Human Services or similar agencies regulate the licensing of child care centers. Specific regulations govern the qualifications of persons who may serve in positions such as Child Care Director, Teacher, Caregiver or Child Care Aide. Requirements for education and experience vary according to the type of position held. All persons who are counted in the staff:child ratio, are required to have physical examinations as well as criminal record checks and statements regarding the status of substance abuse treatment. These are found in the child care licensing standards and regulations booklets.

Interview committees should list qualities and skills which they desire in a candidate who would be offered a position. In addition to any licensing requirements, the list may include personal qualities which could be determined from the statements of references and at the on-site interview. In addition to qualifications of education and experience, the board may want to list such personal attributes as:

Maturity	**Self-confidence**
Enthusiasm	**Warmth**
Flexibility	**Organization**
Dependability	**Ability to "Think on his/her feet"**
Positive role model	**Effective communication skills**
Interest in school-age children	**Uses positive child guidance**

In addition, the Child Care Director should have the ability to:

Make decisions
Supervise and evaluate child care aides
Handle emergency situations effectively
Perform administrative functions including planning and record keeping
Communicate effectively with parents, the board, and school staff
Plan and carry out activities which meets the developmental needs of children

FAIR HIRING PROCEDURES

The board should maintain a file which documents the recruitment process. Entries in the file should include:

A list or statement of recruitment procedures
The job description for the position being hired
A list of the qualifications being sought by the board
All applications submitted
Interview questions
Interview evaluation sheets
A copy of the contract and Staff Handbook
Copies of letters of rejection
Ratings and comments regarding candidates interviewed
The report of committee recommendations

As a part of fair hiring practices, the interviewing process should be standardized as much as possible. Among these considerations are:

The same persons, using a list of standard questions, should conduct all interviews.

The committee may not ask questions which discriminate against classes protected by federal or state law. In most states, employers may not discriminate as to: race, creed, color, national origin, age, ancestry, physical handicaps, marital status or sex.

The committee may not ask about an arrest record. the required criminal and child abuse record checks will catch any offenses that would be unacceptable in child care situations.

Each interview should be concluded with a brief evaluation session. This will allow members individually and as a group, to rate the applicant, while the visit is fresh in mind.

JOB DESCRIPTIONS AND TERMS OF EMPLOYMENT

Clear job descriptions and terms of employment are necessary for hiring staff. Descriptions and terms of employment should be determined prior to interviewing applicants. These written statements should be well understood by the board, as well as any person employed to service the description.

Some boards mail a copy of the appropriate job description, along with a letter of acknowledgement to all persons who submit applications for available positions. Others mail copies of the description only upon request, or to persons who are chosen as candidates.

Model job descriptions and terms of employment may be found in the Staff Handbook (Section G) of this manual.

APPLICATION FORMS

As a matter of equal opportunity practice, boards should require the use of a standard application form. The form should request all information required of staff by the licensing regulations. Use of standard forms will also assist boards in the process of determining which applicants may become candidates.

Model director and aide application forms are available in the Form Book (Section I) of this manual. The Child Care Aide form requests additional information regarding availability, in the case that the aide does not work all of the program hours.

Most minimum standards require the Child Care Director be on-site during regular program hours, however, aide schedules may vary, as long as the staff:child ratio required by the license is always maintained. The application forms should also fulfill licensing requirements for specific information which must be kept in staff record files.

In addition to this information, boards may also request a personal statement from the applicant regarding his or her interest in seeking a child care position, what special skills and talents he/she would bring to the jobs, and why he/she might be especially qualified. The statement could be in a narrative or free text form, or, more specific answers might be requested by one or more printed questions.

ADVERTISING STAFF OPENINGS

Attracting qualified candidates is the first step in hiring staff.   Advertising will help the board to attract the attention of potential candidates. The following methods of recruitment have been effective: classified advertisements in local newspapers and advertisers, college or university newspapers, student employment departments, education and child development departments at nearby colleges or universities, and the state job service agency. In addition to advertisements, programs may recruit from the list of persons who serve as substitute teachers in the school system.

SAMPLE NEWSPAPER ADVERTISEMENTS:

Child Care Director: Washington Elementary School Before & After School Program. Hours Mon. - Fri. 6:50 AM - 8:30 AM, 2:50 PM - 6:00 PM. Experience & education related to school-age children required. E.O.E. $10.00/hour. 351-0050

Child Care Aide: Washington Elementary School Before & After School Program. Hours Mon. - Fri. 6:50 AM - 8:30 AM, 2:50 PM - 6:00 PM. Experience & education related to school-age children preferred. E.O.E. $5.50/hour. 351-0050

SAMPLE RECRUITMENT FLYER:

CHILD CARE STAFF

Child Care staff needed for Before & After School Program located at Washington Elementary School.

Requirements: Experience with school-age children required. A background in early childhood or elementary education, recreation or a child-related field preferred.

Hours: Mornings -   6:45 am to 8:30 am
             Afternoons - 2:45 am to 6:00 pm

Salary: $5.50 - $10.00 per hour, depending on position hired

For Applications and Additional Information Contact: Sam Richard, (319) 351-0500

AN EQUAL OPPORTUNITY EMPLOYER

CHECKING REFERENCES

While it is suggested that applicants have their references forwarded to the board at the time of application, it is essential to check or contact references by phone or written form. A sample reference check form has been attached to these materials. A reference check form is available at the end of this chapter.

Ask questions of the reference person which are related to the list of attributes and qualifications which you are seeking in a candidate for the position being offered. When a reference is interviewed by phone, the reference check form may be used. The interviewer should indicate that the contact was made by phone, sign it and add the time and date. Long-distance time and charges may also recorded on the form.

If a reliable reference which is negative is received, the committee should determine its effect on the applicant's eligibility. If you receive a reference which you're not sure about, express your concerns to the applicant and give him/her a chance to respond.

INTERVIEWING PROCESS

The interview committee will screen applications to develop a list of candidates who will be interviewed such as the model questions later in this section. The applications should be sorted according to the list of qualifications determined by the board, at the outset of the process. Those persons selected for an interview should receive a copy of the Staff Handbook prior to the interview.

OFFERING A CONTRACT

As soon as a decision has been reached, the committee should report to a special meeting of the entire board of directors, regarding their recommendation. The committee should review with the board the procedures followed in recruiting, obtaining information and references, and assessing candidates for a position. Specific information about the finalist should be given.

Following board approval, in order that no time be wasted, a representative should contact the finalist, as soon as possible, by telephone. Upon acceptance, a contract should be offered.

After the contract has been signed, the board should notify any other persons who were interviewed, that the position has been filled. The board may wish to ask these persons if they would be available to serve the program as a substitute when needed.

The Staff Handbook and contracts are interrelated documents. The model contracts appear in the Form Book (Section I) and the Terms of Employment as well as other information appear in the Staff Handbook (Section G) of this manual.

CRIMINAL RECORDS CHECKS AND HEALTH STATEMENTS

According to the law, programs may not seek to obtain confidential information regarding criminal records or the status of the applicant's health and treatment for substance abuse, until a board has determined that a job offer will be made. Criminal records check forms can be obtained your state's child care licensing agency. Upon hiring a caregiver, this form should be completed and submitted without delay. Permanent hirings are dependent on satisfactory results of the checks. A form for the physical examination, as well as substance abuse statements is provided in the Form Book (Section I.)

OPENING A PERSONNEL FILE

Staff information should be placed in individual file folders. The staff member's application form and reference checks should be entered first.

Information required to be in each staff file is listed on the Staff File Checklist Form. Many programs attach the checklist form to the inside of the file folder, facing the folder contents. Additionally the receipt of required information should be recorded on the Composite Staff Information Form. Use of this form is for the convenience of the program in determining completeness of all records. Model Staff File Checklist and Composite Staff Information forms are found in the Form Book (Section I) of this manual.

Each employee should have access to any information about him/herself in program records, with the exception of any confidential employment references. They should have the right to know how such information is being used. A comprehensive list of all documents to be kept in a staff folder is located in the Staff Handbook (Section G) of this manual.

REFERENCE REQUEST

To: _____   Date: _____
Address: _____
City _____
State and Zip _____

From: Sam Richard, Washington Elementary School
       Before & After School Program
       3434 BriarRose
       River City, Iowa 50040

_____ has listed you as a reference in his/her application for a position
as a child care (Circle)   director   child care aide   in the Before and After School Program at
Washington Elementary School. Please fill out and return this form as quickly as possible, so we may
process the application.

REFERENCE

Relationship to Applicant: _____

Dates Associated with Applicant: from: _____   to: _____

How would you rate the applicant's effectiveness in a child care setting?
_____Unacceptable _____Fair _____Good _____Excellent

How would you rate the applicant's dependability in a work situation?
_____Unacceptable _____Fair _____Good _____Excellent

Comments:
_____
_____
_____
_____

_____   _____
Date   Signature of Reference Respondent

INTERVIEW QUESTIONS
FOR DIRECTOR/AIDE CANDIDATES

1.   Describe your child care experience and any special skills which you would bring to this position.

2.   What are your strengths related to child care? Are there any areas in which you would like to have help?

3.   How do you think children are affected by before and after school child care?

4.   How can a before and after school-age child care program complement, but not duplicate the activities which occur during the regular school day.

5.   How would you work with children whose ages may range from 5 to 12, whose developmental abilities may vary widely?

6.   If children fight, how do you respond? Would you intervene? At what point?

7.   How do you feel about name-calling? What would you do if you heard a child make a discriminatory slur?

8.   How might you communicate with program parents regarding their child's experiences in the program? How would you communicate regarding problem behavior?

9.   Describe any experience you have had supervising staff.

10.   Would you be available to work for this program for more than one school year?

11.   What would you like to know about our organization and child care program?

INTERVIEW EVALUATION

Applicant:_____

Position:_____

Interviewer:_____

Date:_____

1. Maturity	1	2	3	4	5
2. Friendliness	1	2	3	4	5
3. Warmth	1	2	3	4	5
4. Responsibility	1	2	3	4	5
5. Communication skills	1	2	3	4	5
6. Attentiveness	1	2	3	4	5
7. Info re child care	1	2	3	4	5
8. Work Experience	1	2	3	4	5
9. Motivation	1	2	3	4	5
10. Organization skills	1	2	3	4	5

Total Score:_____

Codes:
1. Excellent
2. Good
3. Average
4. Below Average
5. Unacceptable

Recommend Hiring: _____Yes   _____No

Please state reasons:

_____

_____

_____

G

BEFORE AND AFTER SCHOOL PROGRAM

POLICIES AND PROCEDURES

STAFF HANDBOOK

TO THE CAREGIVER

As a caregiver, you have a very important role in the growth and development of the children with whom you work. They look to you for guidance and use you as a role model for their emotional, behavioral and social growth. The children's welfare and safety are in your hands.

The Board of Directors is pleased to have you on our staff. We appreciate the time and effort you exert as you work with the children, in order to make the Before and After School Program a safe, happy place for children.

The Staff Handbook is a valid part of the contract between the Before and After School Program and its employees. Any additional duties or agreements between an employee and the Board of Directors, which are not delineated in Sections 100 and 200 of this handbook, must be in writing, signed, dated and attached to all copies of the employee's contract. Additional duties or modifications of the information in Sections 100 and 200 of the Staff Handbook will become binding only after adoption, delivery to staff, and after evidenced in writing, signed and dated by the staff member and President of the Board of Directors. This information must be attached to all copies of the employee's contract. Staff contracts will be subject to additions or modifications in Sections 300 - 600 of this handbook, effective 30 days after their adoption and delivery of a copy to affected staff members.

THE BEFORE AND AFTER SCHOOL PROGRAM
BOARD OF DIRECTORS

TABLE OF CONTENTS

SECTION 100 JOB DESCRIPTIONS

101 Child Care Director

General:

1. Provide a nurturing environment for the supervision of approximately 30 children.
2. Arrive at the child care site at least 10 minutes before the children arrive each day.
3. Remain at the child care site until the last child is gone and the child care area has been put in order according to the expectations for the space as outlined in the Space/Equipment Agreement.
4. Maintain an orderly physical environment conducive to optimal growth and development of children.

Activities Program:

5. Plan and conduct daily activities for the children in the Program that contribute to the care, growth and development of the children who attend the Program. Maintain a daily activities plan book.
6. Prepare materials required to implement the daily activity plans.
7. Manage the distribution and collection of games and materials used in activities.
8. According to Program budget and planning, purchase supplies and equipment for use with children.
9. Schedule resource people who will provide special programs.

Administrative:

10. Keep daily attendance and afternoon child release records; report absences in accordance with Board policy.
11. Collect fees, maintain records of fee payments and convey fees and information to the Board Treasurer.
12. In the case of staff absence, find substitute personnel as needed to replace staff. Provide a schedule of the day's activities for reference of the sub.
13. Schedule assignments of program aides and volunteer personnel.
14. Plan, purchase supplies, supervise service and record daily afternoon nutritious snack.
15. Distribute registration and enrollment forms. Enroll children admitted to the program.
16. Maintain current waiting list of children waiting for enrollment.
17. Keep current, orderly and complete files of required child/staff records according to the licensing specifications for information and location of record keeping.
18. According to Program budget, purchase administrative supplies for use in record keeping.
19. Keep all required postings current.
20. Supervise the purchase of supplies and equipment for the program. Keep accurate records of purchases and inventories of supplies and permanent equipment.

Communication:

21. Maintain a responsible discipline policy and report persistent behavior problems to the Board of Directors, as outlined in the section on Discipline and Discharge.

22.   Communicate regularly with the Board of Directors and the building principal to discuss issues regarding the program.

23.   Prepare reports for and attend Board and Parent meetings. Reports should include specific information on enrollment, purchases of supplies and equipment, collection of fees, snacks, activities, special programming, anticipated needs of the program, behavior problems, and staffing.

Supervisory:

24.   Supervise child care aides and volunteers assigned to assist with activities.

25.   Participate in the evaluation of staff supervised.

Health & Safety:

26.   Be present in the child care room with the children at all times during program hours except in the case of an emergency.

27.   Follow licensing and school procedures to safeguard the health and safety of the children in the Program, which include but are not limited to hand washing, sanitary measures, playground safety rules, rules regarding the use of supplies and equipment.

28.   Become knowledgeable of the emergency file and emergency procedures.

29.   Maintain current, written plans and diagrams for use in case of fire or tornado which will be posted by all exits. Plan, implement and supervise a schedule of required fire and tornado drills.

30.   Hold current certificates in CPR, First Aid, and two hour Child Abuse Reporting Training Session certificate.

31.   Maintain current, written procedures for the storage, recording and administration of medications.

32.   Maintain a current, written plan for medical emergencies and keep staff informed of it, so that it may be implemented as needed in case of emergency.

Professional:

33.   Attend required 6 hours of professional growth annually.

34.   Oversee staff requirement and reporting of attendance at 6 hours of required professional growth.

102 Child Care Aide

1.　Assist the Child Care Director as directed.

2.　Supervise play activities as requested by Child Care Director by:
　　a. participating with children in group games
　　b. enforcing safety rules
　　c. intervening when children are likely to injure themselves or each other
　　d. remaining with the children at all times

3.　Assist in the preparation and maintenance of Program materials as requested by the Child Care Director.

4.　Communicate with the Child Care Director regarding difficult individual child behavior.

5.　Assist the children with self-care activities.

6.　Assist with afternoon snack service.

7.　Attend required 6 hours of professional growth annually.

8.　Be present in the child care room with the children at all times during program hours except in the case of an emergency.

9.　Follow licensing and school procedures to safeguard the health and safety of the children in the Program, which include but are not limited to hand washing, sanitary measures, playground safety rules, and rules regarding the use of supplies and equipment.

10.　Become knowledgeable of the emergency file and emergency procedures.

11.　Know the tornado and fire procedures for the Program, schedule and assist in the supervision of required drills.

12.　Hold a current first aid certificate and a two hour Child Abuse Reporting Training Session certificate.

SECTION 200 TERMS OF EMPLOYMENT

210 PROCESS OF EMPLOYMENT

1.   A written position description including terms of employment as well as personnel policies, will be available to all applicants for their review prior to employment.
2.   Any written notices or advertisements will state the Program's commitment to equal employment opportunity.
3.   Staffing is based on yearly needs and according to the limitations of the Program budget. Contracts will be issued on the basis of one school calendar year.
4.   Any additions or changes in the staff handbook will be presented to each staff member at least ten working days prior to the offering a new contract.

202 PERSONAL PRIVACY

1.   Each employee shall have access to any information about him/herself in Program records, except confidential employment references, and shall have the right to know how such information is being used.
2.   Each employee shall have the opportunity to record what he/she deems to be corrections to the records.

203 EMPLOYEE RECORDS

A confidential personal folder shall be maintained for each employee and shall contain the following information:

1.   Employment application letter and forms
2.   References
3.   An Employment Eligibility Verification Form
4.   A statement signed by the employee that there has been no conviction by any law of any state involving lascivious acts with a child, child neglect or child abuse
5.   A statement signed by the employee concerning the status of any current treatment of alcoholism, drug abuse, or child abuse
6.   A current physical examination report signed by a physician
7.   A copy of Child Day Care Staff Criminal Records Check form and Department of Public Safety Check form
8.   A copy of Request for Child Abuse Information form
9.   A certification of a minimum of two hours of training relating to the identification and reporting of child abuse, and certification of a minimum of two hours of additional training every five years
10.   A professional growth and development form which shall document a minimum attendance of six hours of in-service training and attendance at a workshops, conferences or college courses which benefit professional growth.
11.   Correspondence relating to the employee
12.   Record of employment and termination dates
13.   Performance evaluation reports
14.   Records of salary adjustments
15.   Record of sick leave earned and used

16.   Records of conferences involving the employee
17.   Information or statements which the employee would like to have contained in the file
18.   Record of exit interview
19.   Requests for references
20.   A W-4 will be kept in the salary records.

204 GRIEVANCE PROCEDURE

Caregivers are encouraged, in a climate of openness and mutual respect, to reconcile their differences with each other. If this effort fails, the Child Care Director will make the decision. In the event that the dispute is between a Child Care Aide(s) and the Child Care Director, the Child Care Director may ask the President of the Board of Directors to resolve the conflict. All caregivers will abide by the President's decision.

205 WORK ADMINISTRATION

The Child Care Director is the chief administrative employee of the Program. He/She reports directly and is responsible to the Board of Directors. All caregivers are required to fit themselves into the work of the Program and handle their work in strict cooperation with the Child Care Director and Board of Directors.

206 SEPARATION PRACTICES

1.   Voluntary Separations: A written termination notice must be presented by the caregiver at least two weeks prior to separation from the program. The notice will be filed in the caregiver's personal file.
2.   Involuntary Separations:
    A.   Involuntary separations due to reorganization, retrenchment of the program, or other circumstances arising out of no fault of the employee, is at the discretion of the Board of Directors. The employment contract may be terminated by either the employee or the Program Board of directors on 10 working days written notice to the other. If the Board of Directors terminates the contract, the employee will be entitled to two weeks pay, from the date of notice.
    B.   Dismissal for cause may take place upon written notice from the Board of Directors. Reasons may be for any of the following:
        a. Unsatisfactory performance
        b. Refusal to do work within his/her job description
        c. Repeated unexcused absences
        d. Incompetence
        e. Such other good cause as may be determined by the Board of Directors
    C.   In the event of dismissal for cause, the Board of Directors may terminate employment without notice; compensation to the employee will be at the discretion of the Board.

207 WAGE AND SALARY INFORMATION

A pay period equals two weeks. Paychecks will be issued monthly by the Treasurer of the Board of Directors on the last Program day of the pay period. Salary payments are subject to legally required withholdings. The Board Treasurer will inform the employee regarding calculation of the paycheck, including amount of deductions each period. Salary increases, if any, are at the discretion of the Program Board of Directors.

207A The Child Care Director will receive his/her salary in ten (10) equal payments. The base salary is computed on an hourly wage for a standard number of hours of Program contact time each month as determined by the Board of Directors. The Child Care Director is responsible for maintaining a record/description of administrative time outside of Program hours, which will be presented to the Board of Directors as a part of his/her monthly report.

207B Child Care Aides And Substitutes are paid an hourly wage which will be logged by the Child Care Director on the monthly payroll time sheet.

2108 PERSONAL LEAVE

208A The Child Care Director may accrue 2 1/2 hours of personal leave per pay period. Personal leave may be used for illness, attendance at conferences for the purpose of professional growth or for other personal reasons. With the exception of illness, personal leave taken for more than two days must be approved by the Board of Directors. Additional leave beyond that accrued by an employee may only be taken with out pay, upon approval from the Board of Directors. Personal leave does not accrue from school year to school year. In the event the director's employment is terminated, the employee shall not be entitled to any compensation from personal leave accrued but not taken. Maternity leave may be taken for a period of no more than three months. No pay is involved. Failure to report to work without securing a qualified substitute or giving notice to the Board of Directors may be considered grounds for dismissal.

208B Child Care Aides do not accrue personal leave. In the event of illness, an aide may request personal leave without pay by giving prompt notice to the Child Care Director. In the case that the aide wishes to take leave without pay for a reason other than illness, he/she should make a prompt, advance request to the child care director who will communicate with the Board of Directors regarding approval or denial on a case-by-case basis. In cases other than illness, the cumulative amount of time missed and the ability to secure a qualified substitute will be factored into approval or denial. Failure to report to work without giving notice to the Child Care Director may be considered grounds for dismissal.

209 STAFF BENEFITS

Worker's Compensation will be paid for each caregiver.

210 PROBATIONARY REQUIREMENT

All new caregivers will serve a probationary period of two months. Following the completion of the probationary period, the employee will be evaluated; the Child Care Director will be evaluated by the Board of Directors, child care aides will be evaluated by the Child Care

Director who will consult with the Board of Directors. Two weeks written notice either from the school or from the caregiver must be given in case of termination by either party. In the event of termination the Board of Directors will compensate the employee only to the date separation. Legally, no reason needs to be given if dismissal occurs during the probationary period.

211 STAFF CONDUCT

1. Smoking by caregivers is expressly not permitted anywhere on the school campus. Cigarettes should not be carried where they are visible to children.

2. Alcohol and drug usage by caregivers is not permitted at anytime while on campus, nor is it permissible to have the odor of such drugs on the breath or person.

3. Confidentiality regarding information about children or their families is essential. At no time during or following employment with the Program may a caregiver discuss information about children, parents or other employees.

4. Personal visitors and personal phone calls should not be received during Program hours, except in case of emergency.

5. Personal business may not be conducted during non-Program hours. Personal business includes, but is not limited to: sitting idly, doing homework, reading, or any other activity that is not directly related to the supervision of children or to Program activities.

6. Corporal punishment, verbal abuse, punishment which is humiliating or frightening, threats, and derogatory remarks about the child or his/her family are not permitted at any time.

212 PERFORMANCE EVALUATIONS

1. New caregivers shall be evaluated within the second month of employment following the probationary period, in order to determine employment status and performance.

2. All caregivers are evaluated annually.

3. Performance evaluations of the Child Care Director will be the responsibility the Board of Directors who will perform the evaluation and hold a conference with the Director.

4. Performance evaluations of the child care aides will be the responsibility of the Child Care Director who will perform the evaluation, hold a conference with the aide and report to the Board of Directors.

5. Verbal and written performance evaluations are also given whenever a problem exists, in order to further communication and bring about conflict resolution.

SECTION 300 PROGRAM POLICIES

301 HOURS OF OPERATION

1.   The Program calendar generally follows the calendar of the school district calendar.

2.   Precise days and hours are determined by the Board of Directors. Daily hours are:
Morning Program: 7:00 am - 8:30 am
Afternoon Program: 3:00 pm - 6:00 pm

3.   Caregivers are expected to arrive at least 15 minutes prior to the opening time.   The Child Care Director shall document late staff arrivals.   Three late arrivals may be grounds for dismissal.

302 AFTERNOON CLOSING TIME

1.   The Program closes at 6:00 PM. Parents whose children remain past 6:00 PM must pay overtime fees as follows:
5 - 15 minutes overtime - $5.00 per child
Each additional 1-15 minutes, $5.00 per child
Late fees are paid directly to the caregiver who must stay late.
2.   Child care services may be withdrawn if three overtime charges occur.
3.   Caregivers are expected to remain after Program hours until all children have been appropriately released and facilities used by the Program have been returned to the condition in which they were found.

303 RELEASE OF CHILDREN

1.   Children will leave the afternoon program according to the instructions written by the parent on the Arrival/Departure Procedures Form. Children will be allowed to leave otherwise, or with persons other than the parent only if permission has been given to the Child Care Director in writing by parent on a Change or Exception Arrival/Departure Procedures Form so that the Program is specifically informed of the time(s), date(s), destination(s) and who will be responsible for the child.
2.   If a child attends extracurricular activities within the period he or she is enrolled in the Program, a Change of Arrival/Departure Procedures Form must be filed with the Child Care Director stating the new schedule of the time(s) of activities, destination and who will be responsible for the child when he/she leaves the program.

304 BREAKFAST AND SNACKS

1.   **Morning Program** - We serve a nutritious breakfast at 7:45 a.m.
2.   **Afternoon Program** - We serve nutritious snacks in the afternoon Program.
3.   Parents who want to provide a treat in honor of a child's birthday should contact the Child Care Director to determine the number of children to be served and plan the date.

305 CHILD'S PERSONAL PROPERTY

1.   Children's personal property, coats, clothing, school bags, etc. must be cleared from the child care room after each session of the program.
2.   Program staff will take any personal property which remains after the session to the school office lost and found box.
3.   Although the staff should attempt to help children stay organized, the Program cannot be responsible for lost personal property.

306 VISITORS AND OBSERVATIONS

1.   Parents and community members who are screened by the director are welcome to observe at the Program.
2.   For liability and supervision reasons visiting children may not participate in activities.

307 SCHEDULED & UNSCHEDULED SCHOOL OPENINGS, DELAYS AND CLOSINGS

1.   **Scheduled No-School Days** - The Board will notify parents in advance whether the Program will be available on scheduled no-school days such as conference days.

2.   **Unscheduled No-School Days** - There will be no Program on days when school is canceled due to water main breaks, heating failure, electrical problems, weather, etc.

3.   **Unscheduled School Delays** - The Program will not be open in the morning if school is delayed due to water main breaks, heating failure, electrical problems, weather, etc.

4.   **Scheduled Early Dismissal Days** - The Board will notify parents in advance whether services will be available on scheduled early dismissal days.

5.   **Unscheduled Early Dismissal Days** - The Program is not available when school is dismissed early due to water main breaks, heating failure, electrical problems, weather.

308 WAITING LIST

When the Program is filled to capacity, the Child Care Director will maintain a current list of children who are waiting to enroll in the Program. The Program requires a completed registration form accompanied by a non-refundable registration fee to maintain a child's eligible status for enrollment.

SECTION 400 HEALTH AND SAFETY

401 HEALTH POLICY

1.   If a child has a known medical condition (asthma, diabetes, seizure disorder, etc.) please be sure that the staff knows what to do if a problem should occur during Program hours. Please make sure that any medication is available on site and that the appropriate forms for its use have been completed.

2.   If a child has any one of the following conditions, the parent should be notified to pick up the child immediately:

   Contagious Disease
   Fever over 100 F
   Vomiting or Diarrhea
   Accident Requiring Medical Attention

3.   In case of accident or illness, parents of the child will be called immediately. In serious cases, the child will be taken to one of the local hospitals by ambulance or emergency vehicle for treatment and the parents will be called as soon as possible.

4.   In order to minimize the spread of infectious disease, all staff shall wash their hands upon arrival at the program, before preparing snack, and after leaving the bathroom. Children shall be required to wash their hands before eating snack.

402 DISTRIBUTION OF MEDICATIONS

1.   Whenever a child is to be given prescription or over-the-counter medicine, the parent must provide the program director a completed, signed medication authorization form to the Child Care Director.

2.   Medication brought to the Program must be provided in the original or a duplicate container, or in a container accompanied by the doctor's instructions for its use.

3.   If medication is to be kept at the Program for treatment of a chronic condition, no more than a one month supply should remain at the Program at any time.

4.   Medication kept at the Program must be stored in a locked container or on a shelf inaccessible to the children.

403 ACCIDENTS

1.   If a child is injured at the Program, child care aides must immediately attend the child and notify the Child Care Director.

2.   The injured child should not be left alone. If the Director is not within access of voice, the aide may send a child to notify him/her.

3.   Appropriate first aide treatment should be given the child during which the Director will evaluate the injury for need of further medical attention or for a call to the child's parents.

4.   If appropriate, the injured child may be moved to a quiet area under supervision.

5.   The staff member who arrived at the scene of the child's injury will fill out an Accident Report Form. The original report will be signed by the parents upon arrival and filed in the Accident File. A legible carbon copy or photocopy of the completed form will be placed in the child's personal folder, and a copy will be sent with the child's parent or the person responsible who arrives to pick up the child.

6.   If a staff member is injured on the job, an incident form must be completed and filed.

404 BUILDING AND PLAYGROUND RULES

An annual conference with the school principal will provide specific information regarding building and playground rules. Program rules must be consistent with school rules.

General rules which must be implemented by Program staff include:

1.   Use of soft, indoor voices, except in the gym or playground
2.   No climbing on school furniture
3.   No running except where permitted in the gym or playground
4.   Appropriate use of Program supplies and equipment
5.   Food will be confined to areas designated for snack preparation and service
6.   Staff and children must remain at all times within the Program facilities
7.   Alert supervision according to correct staff:children ratio at all times
8.   Appropriate use of any building signal for restoring quiet
9.   Children are never allowed to move, touch or ride on a TV/VCR cart
10. Children are never allowed to move, set up or take down movable lunchroom tables
11. The building custodian is to be called in the event of need for sanitary clean up of body fluids.

405 ABSENCES

If a child will not be attending the Program because of scheduled appointment, vacations, or other planned absences, the parent should notify the Child Care Director in advance. If a child is ill, when the parent calls the school to report the illness or comes to pick up the child from school, he or she should request the school secretary to put a notice of the child's absence in the Program mailbox.

If a child does not arrive at the program as intended, the Child Care Director will contact the parents. If the parents cannot be reached, the Director will contact the child's emergency persons.

406 OUTDOOR PLAY

The children will not be allowed to play outdoors when the temperature (including wind chill) falls below 0 degrees Fahrenheit.

407 FIREARMS ON THE CAMPUS

In the case of someone appearing on the premises with a firearm, the emergency number (911) should be called and the children taken out of danger and given aide as needed as quickly as possible.

408 PARENT UNDER THE INFLUENCE OF DRUGS OR ALCOHOL

Caregivers are to make every effort to keep a child from getting into a car with a parent under the influence of drugs or alcohol. They should call the police to give the child and parent a ride home. Caregivers should not under any circumstances give transportation to a parent who appears to be impaired by drugs or alcohol because the Program insurance does not cover transportation related to the Program. If a child is removed from the program by a parent who appears to be under the influence, caregivers are to make every attempt to copy the car license number and notify the authorities.

409 MANDATORY REPORTING OF CHILD ABUSE

The Department of Human Services requires caregivers to report suspected cases of child abuse. This includes the reporting of parents who appear to be impaired by drugs or alcohol.

500 DISCIPLINE AND DISCHARGE

501. DISCIPLINE

It is the goal of the Before and After School Program to provide a supportive environment in which children can grow and develop. Positive child guidance management methods are used in this program.

502. DISCHARGE

Children are entitled to a pleasant and harmonious environment at the Program. The Before and After School Program cannot serve children whose display chronically disruptive behavior.

Chronically disruptive behavior is defined as verbal or physical activity which may include but is not limited to such behavior that: requires constant attention from the staff, inflicts of physical or emotional harm on other children, abuses the staff, ignores or disobeys the rules which guide behavior during the school day and Program time. If a child cannot adjust to the rules of the Program setting and behave appropriately, then the child may be discharged.

Reasonable efforts will be made to assist children to adjust to the Program setting. Disruptive behavior will be dealt with in the following manner:

1. The misbehaving child will be given a five minute time-out, in order for him/her to cool off and think about his/her actions.
2. If a second, 10 minute time-out is given to the child in a single day, a incident report will be written by the caregiver. This report is to be given to the parent or guardian to read and sign. The report will be returned to the caregiver where it will remain with the child's enrollment information.

3.   If a child receives three written behavior-related reports, the child will be suspended effective at the end of the day of the third report. During the first week of the suspension, the parents, caregiver and a member of the Board of Directors, other than the child's parent, will meet in a conference setting in order to determine the conditions for reinstatement. **Parents will be responsible for the payment of tuition during the period of suspension or until the child is withdrawn from the Program or is discharged by action of the Board of Directors. Tuition and refund policies shall be as set out in Section 603 Fees, of this handbook.**

4.   If the child is reinstated in the program and receives a fourth behavior-related report, the director may suspend the child immediately, including if necessary, notifying the parent to come and get the child. The director may make such recommendations to the Board of Directors as are appropriate, including discharge without the right of reinstatement. The director will bring this to the prompt attention of the Board of Directors who will act upon the recommendations of the director regarding continuation of the child in the program. **Parents will continue to be responsible for the payment of tuition during the period of suspension or until the child is withdrawn from the Program or is discharged by action of the Board of Directors, who will notify the parent. Tuition and refund policies shall be as set out in Section 603 Fees.**

5.   If the severity of a problem is great enough that it could endanger the safety of the child or other children in the Program, discharge will be effective immediately after the director consults with the Board of Directors who will notify the parent.

600 FINANCIAL POLICIES

601 COLLECTION OF MONIES BY THE DIRECTOR:
1.   The Child Care Director is responsible for all monies collected at the Program.
2.   In the event of his/her absence, the Director will designate a staff person to collect money on the day of absence.
3.   Money should be collected in a transmittal envelope which be should conveyed at the end of the day to the Board Treasurer.

602 PURCHASING, REIMBURSEMENT AND VOUCHERS:
1.   Guided by the Program operating budget, the Child Care Director will make purchases of supplies and equipment for use in the Program.
2.   The Director will record the check number, write a brief explanation of the purchases, and attach the store receipt to an initialed voucher form, which will be transmitted to the Board Treasurer. The Board Treasurer will provide financial oversight of the Director's use of Program checks.
3.   In the event of an odd purchase, when the Director does not have a program check, a voucher form may be completed, indicating the need for reimbursement. Except for rare occasions, the Director will not use personal funds to purchase program supplies.

603 FEES

The Program salaries, supplies and administrative expenses are supported entirely by fees. The River City Community School district provides the space, utilities and custodial services as an in-kind donation to the Program.

1.   The registration fee is a non-refundable fee.

2.   Tuition payments are due the first school day of each month and are paid to reserve an entire month of child care, according to the option agreement, irrespective of the actual number of days and/hours the child attends the Program.

3.   Any tuition that is not paid by the last day of the first full week of the month in which it is due will result in an immediate suspension of child care services until the fees are paid in full. If the tuition is not paid in full by the end of the second full week the child shall be automatically discharged from the Program. Reinstatement may occur on a space-available basis when all fees have been paid.

4.   Nonsufficient fund checks are held until a cash or money order is received by the Program to cover the amount of the check. Parents will pay a $10.00 charge for a NSF check. Parents will be notified immediately upon receipt of the NSF notice by the program and shall have two school days in which to pay the charge and tuition in full by cash or equivalent. If not paid by the end of the second day after notice, child care services will be suspended immediately. If the tuition and charge is not paid in full by the end of the first full week after notice, the child will be discharged from the program.

5.   If a child withdraws or is discharged from the Program, tuition will be due for the balance of the month or for one-half month, which ever amount is greater.

6.   If all of the child's required enrollment forms are not completed and returned to the Child Care Director by the day the child is scheduled to start the Program, the child will not be allowed to attend until these completed forms are submitted to the Child Care Director. The parent/guardian/ custodian **will be responsible for payment of monthly fees from starting from that date in order to reserve the enrollment spot until such time as the completed forms are returned.** These forms include: the Enrollment Form, the Arrival/Departure Form, the Release Form, the Parental Emergency Medical Consent Form, the Registration Agreement, and a Physical Assessment Form (if one is not available in the child's school folder).

BEFORE AND AFTER SCHOOL PROGRAM

A STATEMENT-BASED APPROACH TO STAFF EVALUATION

A STATEMENT-BASED APPROACH TO
STAFF EVALUATION

The Challenge of Staff Evaluation

The central goals of staff evaluation are to maintain a stable and nurturing environment for the children who are served by the program, and to support staff development. However, staff evaluation is a challenge for many child care boards and their staff members. Among other factors contributing to this is the variety of work roles carried out by staff in a school-age child care center. Staff evaluation procedures must consider these roles, and should be adaptable to the characteristics of the particular role of the child care director or aide, such as the following considerations:

Child Care Directors are responsible for the formidable task of planning and implementing daily activities for the programs. They plan these activities from a variety of resources, not the least, personal talents, skills and creativity.

Since the board members are also parents of children enrolled in the program, this is often a source of unspoken tension between the board and staff.

Staff must manage programs for children who may vary greatly in age and developmental abilities.

Staff job descriptions may entail a wide range of duties in addition to supervising the children. They may be responsible for the supervision of aides, clerical functions, food purchasing, preparation, service, and clean-up, as well as light maintenance of the facility.

Caregivers have frequent personal contact with program parents. They are expected to communicate about the child, collect tuition and to enforce program policies and procedures.

Boards and staff need to accept that meaningful and accurate evaluation requires a commitment of time. Use of an evaluation model based on the caregiver's job description and performance statements often eases the tension, and negative feelings which are associated with evaluations.

Several assumptions form the foundation of the following procedures: It is assumed that a basic trust exists between parent board members and their children's caregivers, that program staff members like the children with whom they work, and that they are capable of professional growth. In order to implement the procedures, each staff member must have an accurate job description on record.

These procedures necessarily involve staff in describing their own work activities. When they participate in this way, they may become more aware of areas in which they would like to develop professionally. Board evaluators often respond to reading the accounts of staff activities, by gaining increased awareness of staff activities and how they relate to the staff job description.

The use of the following procedures can improve the usefulness and quality of staff evaluations, while at the same time, improving staff satisfaction with the evaluation process. The evaluation will be based on information which is meaningful in the context of each caregiver's job description. Given the nature of work in a school-age program, more general techniques of evaluation are inappropriate.

Involving Staff in the Evaluation Process

Staff must have confidence that their evaluations are based on information which is accurate and related to their job descriptions. Use of an evaluation model in which staff participate increases staff perception of fairness. When they become active partners in their own evaluation, they are more likely to support the outcome and respond with constructive towards desired change.

For these reasons, the use of performance statements provide a manageable and genuine means of involving staff in their evaluations. A performance statement is just a record of something the staff member has done:

> "Wrote and supervised the use of two word searches about pets."
> "Called Ann M's mom to discuss how to deal with her headaches."

Performance statements do not evaluate how well something was done, ie: "Did a good job of parent education." Performance statements simply describe what was done.

What Are Appropriate Statements?

Successful use of this approach depends on an understanding of appropriate performance statements, as well as the ability to record them according to their corresponding categories.

Performance statements may be brief. They need not be complete sentences. They do not use words or phrases state "how well" the staff member believes something was done. Statements should objectively describe what was done. Information given may be general or give specific information about numbers, amounts, time duration and other details, to provide more accurate information.

Child Care Directors can create performance statements during the course of a normal day. The Child Care Director's board reports, phone notes and messages, shopping lists, or activity plans can produce performance statements. Calendar notes, activity records, copies of letters to parents, handouts from professional growth inservices are additional examples of performance statements.

Collecting Performance Statements

The staff member to be evaluated must know and understand the general categories from the job description or other sources, on which the evaluation will be based.

Staff members are responsible for collecting statements which describe their performance. The staff member should to note information about their activities and systematically write it down. The information may be coded, or recorded according to the category.

Staff members should be encouraged to gather information and record performance statements **on a regular basis.** Some child care directors write a brief summary of the day's or week's activities and post it beside the sign-out sheet to let parents know what went on during that time. Those caregivers might file those notes as evidence that he or she has "Plans and Conducts Developmentally Appropriate Activities." Those notes might also contain information which would provide information in other categories. When recorded, statements should be dated.

Methods of gathering statements vary according to the preference of the program board and staff. Some programs provide forms in categorical files; others prefer a three ring notebook with index or pocket pages labeled with the category. Others drop notes into a file and periodically sort and record them. Ideally, this would occur once per week to provide for maximum recall. Whatever the method, it must be made "user-friendly" and easy to expand as needed. The board may want to give guidance to staff regarding the number which they consider to be a desirable frequency or number of entries. Child care directors who supervise aides may wish to assign a time for aides to record statements.

Before the evaluation conference, each staff member should review his or her performance statements and complete the pre-conference form. Use of the statements should facilitate the recording of more specific information, than if the person had relied upon memory alone.

The Evaluation Process

Evaluation is a process involving five steps:

1.   **Self-monitoring by staff; recording performance statements**
2.   **Monitoring of the staff by person(s) involved in evaluating**
3.   **Pre-Evaluation Activities**
4.   **The Evaluation Conference**
5.   **The Post-Evaluation Summary**

The evaluation is an ongoing process, not an annual event. The purposes are to promote a dialogue on job performance and to support staff development.

1.   Self-monitoring by Staff:

The importance of regular monitoring must be reinforced if the evaluation is to cover more that just the last few weeks. We tend to remember major events, particularly the disasters, but day-to-day activities and many of the successes are often lost.

Psychologists have a name for what usually happens. They call it the "Recency Effect," and the "Santa Claus Effect." "Recency" says that we remember best what our employees did last week, and our perception of what they did five months ago is flavored by those recent events. The "Santa Claus Effect" says that employees tend to make their best efforts right before they are evaluated. These two effects may distort accurate evaluation.

2.   Monitoring by Person(s) Involved in Evaluating:

Some boards and child care directors find it useful to meet with their employees on a regular basis with a prepared agenda ("to review the month and talk about next month's programming, snack schedule, etc.) covering the caregiver's current and projected activities. The supervising person should provide the caregiver with the agenda (even if it is an informal note) and the time should be planned for the convenience of both persons.

The supervising person should make notes (dated) of the conversation and retain them in a file. This file should be open to review by the employee. The supervising person will use the notes to keep track of and follow up ongoing issues and concerns.

3.   Pre-Evaluation Activities:

The purpose of pre-evaluation activities is to prevent surprises to both the supervisor and the employee, and to promote two-way communication. The process may look like this:

1.   At least two weeks before the evaluation conference, the supervisor schedules a time for the conference with the employee and asks him or her to organize and summarize his or her performance statements on a pre-conference form.

2.   A few days prior to the conference, the employee should give the pre-conference form to the supervisor.

3.   The supervising person should fill out a pre-conference performance form.

4. The Evaluation Conference:

The evaluation conference should be scheduled for a place and time which will allow for adequate time for uninterrupted conversation. The agenda should include the use of the caregiver's performance statements, information from the employee's pre-conference form and the supervisor's pre-conference form.

1.   Both the employee and supervisor should have a copy of the Staff Handbook, which contains the job description and related program information.

2.   Employee and supervisor should first cover the issues on the employee's pre-conference form other than those related to performance statements.

3.   Next, the employee's review factors should be covered. This should be a dialogue about actual performance covered under the evaluation categories. The supervisor should expand on both positives and negatives of the performance in order to increase understanding of expectations. The supervisor should cover the factors which went into his or her rating in each category. Should the supervisor change any of his or her ratings based on the dialogue, this should be noted.

4.   The supervisor should be prepared to describe any developmental needs and suggest ways the employee supervisor might become more effective. The supervisor might also anticipate ways in which he, she, or the board might assist the employee.

5. The Post-Evaluation Summary:

After the conference, the supervisor should complete the Post-Evaluation form, which will be placed in the employee's file attached to the two pre-conference forms. To finalize the process:

1.   The employee should have an opportunity to add written comments to the Post-Evaluation Form.

2.   Both the employee and supervisor should sign the final evaluation form. Signing the form acknowledges that the conference took place, not necessarily agreement with the evaluation.

Summary

After an evaluation, the caregiver and supervisor should turn to those needs identified in the conference and make efforts to achieve the corresponding goals for the next evaluation cycle.

Evaluation based on performance statements supports and protects both the caregivers and the Board of Directors. Since staff are more aware of their own performance, they are more likely to cooperate with any plans or changes resulting from the evaluation. Since the Board of Directors becomes more aware of the activities of the caregivers, it is in a better position to appreciate and constructively support the staff members who care for their children.

The following forms illustrate the evaluation process. They are written within the context of the job descriptions written in the Staff Handbook.

> **Evaluator's Pre-Conference Form for Director**
> **Evaluator's Pre-Conference Form for Aide**
> **Director Pre-Conference Form**
> **Aide Pre-Conference Form**
> **Director Post Evaluation Summary**
> **Aide Evaluation Summary**

Caregiver:_____   Evaluator(s):_____

Evaluator Pre-Conference Form
CHILD CARE DIRECTOR
PERFORMANCE EVALUATION
for the period
_____ to _____

The Evaluation Process

A.   The purposes of staff evaluation are to:
Identify caregiver strengths as well as developmental needs.
Provide an opportunity for two-way communication.
Accomplish a fair appraisal of the previous period performance.

B.   The purpose of this form is to provide for pre-evaluation. Please complete it prior to the date of the Evaluation Conference on: (date)_____.

C.   At the Evaluation Conference, the caregiver and supervisor will discuss evaluation issues. After the Conference, the supervisor will complete a Post-Evaluation Summary. Both will sign the final evaluation form. Signing the form acknowledges that the conference took place, not necessarily agreement with the evaluation.

FACTORS FOR REVIEW

Please rate the caregiver's performance in each area of the Factors for Review. If you change any of these ratings as a result of the Evaluation Conference dialogue, please note these changes. Make any notes next to the factor ratings.

1. Attendance & Punctuality
1. ____Exceeds Expectations
2. ____Meets Expectations
3. ____Improvement Desirable
4. ____Improvement Essential

2. Maintains Physical Environment and Equipment
1. ____Exceeds Expectations
2. ____Meets Expectations
3. ____Improvement Desirable
4. ____Improvement Essential

3. Maintains Positive, Nurturing Environment
1. ____Exceeds Expectations
2. ____Meets Expectations
3. ____Improvement Desirable
4. ____Improvement Essential

Evaluator Pre-Conference Form, Page 2
CHILD CARE DIRECTOR
PERFORMANCE EVALUATION

Name of Caregiver_____

4. Plans and Conducts Developmentally Appropriate Activities
1. ____Exceeds Expectations
2. ____Meets Expectations
3. ____Improvement Desirable
4. ____Improvement Essential

5. Keeps Accurate Records as Required by the Board and Licensing
1. ____Exceeds Expectations
2. ____Meets Expectations
3. ____Improvement Desirable
4. ____Improvement Essential

6. Uses and Models Developmentally Appropriate Behavior Management Practices
1. ____Exceeds Expectations
2. ____Meets Expectations
3. ____Improvement Desirable
4. ____Improvement Essential

7. Effective Communications With Parents
1. ____Exceeds Expectations
2. ____Meets Expectations
3. ____Improvement Desirable
4. ____Improvement Essential

8. Effective Communications With Other Staff
1. ____Exceeds Expectations
2. ____Meets Expectations
3. ____Improvement Desirable
4. ____Improvement Essential

9. Effective Communications With Principal and Building Staff
1. ____Exceeds Expectations
2. ____Meets Expectations
3. ____Improvement Desirable
4. ____Improvement Essential

Evaluator Pre-Conference Form, Page 3
CHILD CARE DIRECTOR
PERFORMANCE EVALUATION

Name of Caregiver_____

10. Record of Professional Growth
1. ____Exceeds Expectations
2. ____Meets Expectations
3. ____Improvement Desirable
4. ____Improvement Essential

11. Performance Not Specified in Factors for Review
1. ____Exceeds Expectations
2. ____Meets Expectations
3. ____Improvement Desirable
4. ____Improvement Essential

Caregiver:_____ Evaluator(s):_____

Evaluator Pre-Conference Form
CHILD CARE AIDE
PERFORMANCE EVALUATION
for the period
_____ to _____

The Evaluation Process

A. The purposes of staff evaluation are to:
Identify caregiver strengths as well as developmental needs.
Provide an opportunity for two-way communication.
Accomplish a fair appraisal of the previous period performance.

B. The purpose of this form is to provide for pre-evaluation. Please complete it prior to the date of the Evaluation Conference on: (date)_____.

C. At the Evaluation Conference, the caregiver and supervisor will discuss evaluation issues. After the Conference, the supervisor will complete a Post-Evaluation Summary. Both will sign the final evaluation form. Signing the form acknowledges that the conference took place, not necessarily agreement with the evaluation.

FACTORS FOR REVIEW

Please rate the caregiver's performance in each area of the Factors for Review. If you change any of these ratings as a result of the Evaluation Conference dialogue, please note these changes. Make any notes next to the factor ratings.

1. Attendance & Punctuality
1. ____Exceeds Expectations
2. ____Meets Expectations
3. ____Improvement Desirable
4. ____Improvement Essential

2. Assists in the Maintenance of the Physical Environment and Equipment
1. ____Exceeds Expectations
2. ____Meets Expectations
3. ____Improvement Desirable
4. ____Improvement Essential

3. Is Actively Involved with the Children in a Positive Manner and Uses Developmentally Appropriate Behavior Management Practices
1. ____Exceeds Expectations
2. ____Meets Expectations
3. ____Improvement Desirable
4. ____Improvement Essential

Evaluator Pre-Conference Form, Page 2
CHILD CARE AIDE
PERFORMANCE EVALUATION

Name of Caregiver_____

4. Enforces Health and Safety Rules and Practices
1. ____Exceeds Expectations
2. ____Meets Expectations
3. ____Improvement Desirable
4. ____Improvement Essential

5. Assists Children With Developmentally Appropriate Activities
1. ____Exceeds Expectations
2. ____Meets Expectations
3. ____Improvement Desirable
4. ____Improvement Essential

6. Effective Communications With Child Care Director
1. ____Exceeds Expectations
2. ____Meets Expectations
3. ____Improvement Desirable
4. ____Improvement Essential

7. Effective Communications With Other Staff
1. ____Exceeds Expectations
2. ____Meets Expectations
3. ____Improvement Desirable
4. ____Improvement Essential

8. Record of Professional Growth
1. ____Exceeds Expectations
2. ____Meets Expectations
3. ____Improvement Desirable
4. ____Improvement Essential

9. Performance Not Specified in Factors for Review
1. ____Exceeds Expectations
2. ____Meets Expectations
3. ____Improvement Desirable
4. ____Improvement Essential

Name_____ Date_____

Staff Pre-Conference Form
CHILD CARE DIRECTOR
PERFORMANCE EVALUATION
for the period
_____ to _____

The Evaluation Process

A.   The purposes of staff evaluation are to:

        Identify caregiver strengths as well as developmental needs.
        Provide an opportunity for two-way communication.
        Accomplish a fair appraisal of the previous period performance.

B.   The purpose of this form is to provide for pre-evaluation input. Please return it to the person who will conduct the review by the date_____.

C.   The date for the Evaluation Conference will be: _____.

D.   Please complete the General Topics questions. You may attach use the back of the form or pages if needed.

E.   Please summarize your performance statements under the categories established as Factors for Review.

F.   At the Evaluation Conference, the caregiver and supervisor will discuss evaluation issues. After the Conference, the supervisor will complete a Post-Evaluation Summary. Both of you will you and your supervisor will sign the final evaluation form. Signing the form acknowledges that the conference took place, not necessarily agreement with the evaluation.

GENERAL TOPICS

1. What are the activities, functions or aspects of your job which you like best?

2. What are the activities, functions or aspects of your job which you like least?

3. Are there any aspects of the child care program which you would like to see changed insofar as they affect your work?

Staff Pre-Conference Form, Page 2
CHILD CARE DIRECTOR
PERFORMANCE EVALUATION

Name of Caregiver_____

4. What aspects of your relationship with your supervisor do you like best?

5. Do you have any suggestions that you would like to make concerning your supervisor that would make your working relationship more effective?

FACTORS FOR REVIEW
   Please summarize your performance statements in each area of the Factors for Review. You may support your summary at the conference with performance statements gathered during the period under review.

1. Attendance & Punctuality-

2. Maintains Physical Environment and Equipment-

3. Maintains Positive, Nurturing Environment-

4. Plans and Conducts Developmentally Appropriate Activities-

5. Keeps Accurate Records as Required by the Board and Licensing-

Staff Pre-Conference Form, Page 3
CHILD CARE DIRECTOR
PERFORMANCE EVALUATION

Name of Caregiver_____

6. Uses and Models Developmentally Appropriate Behavior Management Practices-

7. Effective Communications With Parents-

8. Effective Communications With Other Staff-

9. Effective Communications With Principal and Building Staff-

10. Record of Professional Growth-

11. Performance Not Specified in Factors for Review:

Name_____   Date_____

Staff Pre-Conference Form
CHILD CARE AIDE
PERFORMANCE EVALUATION
for the period
_____ to _____

The Evaluation Process

A.   The purposes of staff evaluation are to:

Identify caregiver strengths as well as developmental needs.
Provide an opportunity for two-way communication.
Accomplish a fair appraisal of the previous period performance.

B.   The purpose of this form is to provide for pre-evaluation input. Please return it to the person who will conduct the review by the date_____.

C.   The date for the Evaluation Conference will be: _____.

D.   Please complete the General Topics questions. You may attach use the back of the form or pages if needed.

E.   Please summarize your performance statements under the categories established as Factors for Review.

F.   At the Evaluation Conference, the caregiver and supervisor will discuss evaluation issues. After the Conference, the supervisor will complete a Post-Evaluation Summary. Both of you will you and your supervisor will sign the final evaluation form. Signing the form acknowledges that the conference took place, not necessarily agreement with the evaluation.

GENERAL TOPICS

1. What are the activities, functions or aspects of your job which you like best?

2. What are the activities, functions or aspects of your job which you like least?

3. Are there any aspects of the child care program which you would like to see changed insofar as they affect your work?

Staff Pre-Conference Form, Page 2
CHILD CARE AIDE
PERFORMANCE EVALUATION

Name of Caregiver_____

4. What aspects of your relationship with your supervisor do you like best?

5. Do you have any suggestions that you would like to make concerning your supervisor that would make your working relationship more effective?

FACTORS FOR REVIEW

Please summarize your performance statements in each area of the Factors for Review. You may support your summary at the conference with performance statements gathered during the period under review.

1. Attendance & Punctuality-

2. Assists in the Maintenance of the Physical Environment and Equipment-

3. Is Actively Involved with the Children in a Positive Manner and Uses Developmentally Appropriate Behavior Management Practices-

4. Enforces Health and Safety Rules and Practices-

5. Assists Children With Developmentally Appropriate Activities-

Staff Pre-Conference Form, Page 3
CHILD CARE AIDE
PERFORMANCE EVALUATION

Name of Caregiver_____

6. Effective Communications With Child Care Director-

7. Effective Communications With Other Staff-

8. Record of Professional Growth-

9. Performance Not Specified in Factors for Review:

Caregiver:_____ Evaluator(s):_____

CHILD CARE DIRECTOR
PERFORMANCE EVALUATION SUMMARY
for the period
_____ to _____

EVALUATOR'S SUMMARY OF STAFF MEMBER'S PERFORMANCE: Insert numerical score (1-4) from Pre-Conference Form, and write a brief comment regarding performance or future development.

1.   Attendance & Punctuality-

2.   Maintains Physical Environment and Equipment-

3.   Maintains Positive, Nurturing Environment-

4.   Plans and Conducts Developmentally Appropriate Activities-

5.   Keeps Accurate Records as Required by the Board and Licensing-

6.   Uses and Models Developmentally Appropriate Behavior Management Practices-

7.   Effective Communications With Parents-

8.   Effective Communications With Other Staff-

9.   Effective Communications With Principal and Building Staff-

10.   Record of Professional Growth-

11.   Performance Not Specified in Factors for Review:

OVERALL EVALUATION: 1. ____**Exceeds Expectations**
                                 2. ____**Meets Expectations**
                                 3. ____**Improvement Desirable**
                                 4. ____**Improvement Essential**

EVALUATOR'S SUMMARY OF DISCUSSION WITH STAFF MEMBER:

STAFF MEMBER'S COMMENTS:

_____   _____
*Staff Member's Signature/Date   Evaluator's Signature/Date
*Signing the form acknowledges that the conference took place, not necessarily agreement with the evaluation.

Caregiver:_____ Evaluator(s):_____

CHILD CARE AIDE
PERFORMANCE EVALUATION SUMMARY
for the period
_____ to _____

EVALUATOR'S SUMMARY OF STAFF MEMBER'S PERFORMANCE: Insert numerical score (1-4) from Pre-Conference Form, and write a brief comment regarding performance or future development.

1.   Attendance & Punctuality-

2.   Assists in the Maintenance of the Physical Environment and Equipment-

3.   Is Actively Involved with the Children in a Positive Manner and Uses Developmentally   Appropriate Behavior Management Practices-

4.   Enforces Health and Safety Rules and Practices-

5.   Assists Children With Developmentally Appropriate Activities-

6.   Effective Communications With Child Care Director-

7.   Effective Communications With Other Staff-

8.   Record of Professional Growth-

9.   Performance Not Specified in Factors for Review-

OVERALL EVALUATION: 1. ____**Exceeds Expectations**
                                     2. ____**Meets Expectations**
                                     3. ____**Improvement Desirable**
                                     4. ____**Improvement Essential**

EVALUATOR'S SUMMARY OF DISCUSSION WITH STAFF MEMBER:

STAFF MEMBER'S COMMENTS:

_____   _____
*Staff Member's Signature/Date   Evaluator's Signature/Date
*Signing the form acknowledges that the conference took place, not necessarily agreement with the evaluation.

I

BEFORE AND AFTER SCHOOL PROGRAM

FORM BOOK

REGISTRATION AND ENROLLMENT POLICIES

Registration: The parent must complete the registration form below and submit it with a $20.00 non-refundable registration fee to the Child Care Director. Children who cannot be immediately enrolled will be placed on a waiting list.

Eligibility: Children in grades K-6 may be registered for enrollment in the program at any time.

Openings: Full and part-time openings are determined on the basis of the number of full time equivalents (FTEs) permitted by the program's license. When full or part-time child care openings occur, parents of registered children are contacted for enrollment on the basis of: 1) the time slot indicated on the registration form, and, 2) on a first-come basis for the time slot according to the date of registration receipt.

Enrollment:
1. Parents will be provided with a set of enrollment forms for each child. All forms must be completed and returned to the Director before the child's first day of attendance.
2. Parents will pay a non-refundable enrollment fee and first month tuition fee befire the child's first day of attendance.
3. Children will be allowed to attend the program only after all forms have been completed and returned, and payments have been submitted.
4. If the parent has not submitted completed forms or payment on the date when the child is scheduled to start attending, the parent will be responsible for payment of monthly fees to reserve the enrollment spot until the completed forms and payment are returned.

_____ (Detach) _____

BEFORE & AFTER SCHOOL PROGRAM REGISTRATION FORM

Child's Name	Date of Birth	Home Phone #

Name of Parent(s)	Address	Work Phone #

Indicate below your first and second choices:
____ Full time mornings and afternoons   ____ Full-time mornings
____ Part-time mornings (Circle) M T W Th F   ____ Full-time afternoons
____ Part-time afternoons (Circle) M T W Th F

I have read and understand the policies above and would like to register my child for enrollment in the program. I have attached the $20.00 non-refundable registration fee.

Parent Signature   Date   School: Date of Receipt of Registration Form and Fee

ENROLLMENT AGREEMENT

1. I understand that I am enrolling my child:_____
for the current school year. He/she will attend:
   _____ Full time mornings and afternoons
   _____ Full-time mornings
   _____ Part-time mornings (Please Circle) M T W Th F
   _____ Full-time afternoons
   _____ Part-time afternoons (Please Circle) M T W Th F

2. I understand that the Program is open according to the official school calendar of the River City Community School District, and is closed during vacations, and inclement weather days.

3. I understand that I am responsible payment of monthly fees in the amount of _____ which are due the school day of each month. I will give 30 days notice in writing prior to withdrawal from the program during which time I will be responsible for payment of fees.

4. I understand that in the event of any absences during program hours, activities, I will be responsible for fees for time reserved, not actual time spent at the Program.

5. I will update my child's file information as outlined in the Parent Handbook.

6. The Program staff will assume full responsibility for my child from the time he/she arrives at the program until my child leaves the program according to the written instructions for departure.

7. If a medical emergency arises, the Program staff will first attempt to contact me. If I cannot be reached, the staff will contact my child's doctor. If the emergency is such that immediate hospital attention is necessary, an ambulance or emergency vehicle may take my child to the hospital.

I agree to adhere to the stated policies and procedures of the Before and After School Program as stated here and in the Parent Handbook, and give my child permission to participate fully in this program.

_____
Date   Signature

_____
        Relationship to Child

Submit this completed statement accompanied by the enrollment fee, first month's fee, and completed enrollment forms to the Child Care Director.

Program Use: Date of receipt_____ First date of attendance_____

ENROLLMENT FORM

1. Child's Identification:

_____

Child's Name   Date of Birth   Sex

_____

Address   Phone Number

If Child does not go by his/her first name, what does he/she prefer to be called? _____

_____

2. Parent(s)/Guardian(s)/Custodian(s) Identification:

1.   _____

Name   Relationship to Child

_____

Address   Home Phone

_____

Employer   Department

_____

Work Phone   Work Hours

Prefer to be contacted first: (Circle) M T W TH F

Child resides with above? (Circle)   Yes   No
Please explain arrangements if applicable:_____

_____

2.   _____

Name   Relationship to Child

_____

Address   Home Phone

_____

Employer   Department

_____

Work Phone   Work Hours

Prefer to be contacted first: (Circle) M T W TH F

Child resides with above? (Circle)   Yes   No
Please explain arrangements if applicable:_____

_____

Parents' Status:
1. Single_____   Married_____   Divorced_____   Separated_____

2. If there is a separation or divorce custody problem of which the Program staff should be aware? If yes, please explain: No____Yes_____

_____

_____

_____

Indicate the name of the person responsible for payment of fees:_____
If different from the name of a parent listed on page 1, complete the following information:

Name_____   Work Phone_____
Address_____   Home Phone_____

Name of a third person, such as a child care provider, if applicable:

Name_____ Relationship to Child_____ Work #_____
Address_____   Home #_____

Emergency Persons:
These should be local persons who may be notified in case of emergency or illness when the above-listed people are not available.

Name_____ Relationship to Child_____ Work #_____
Address_____   Home #_____
Name_____ Relationship to Child_____ Work #_____
Address_____   Home #_____

Name_____ Relationship to Child_____ Work #_____
Address_____   Home #_____

4.   Release of Child:
May child leave the Program with the persons listed above in sections 1,2, and 3? (Please check below)

_____ Yes, he/she may depart with any of the persons listed.
_____ No, he/she may not leave with the following persons (Include persons not above listed):

_____

_____

_____

5.   Medical Information:

1. Allergies (food, medication, bees)_____

2. Chronic or recurrent illnesses or disorders:_____
_____
_____

3. Does your child take medication for #2 above? If yes, please state the name and dosage.
_____
_____

4. Will the medication need to be given during program hours? If yes, when will it need to be given? No_____ Yes_____ _____
_____
_____

5. What should we do if your child has a problem related to his/her medical condition during program hours?_____
_____
_____

6.   Child's Information:
1. Other siblings in the home:

Name	Birth Date	Enrolled in Program?

2. Does your child have any eating problems or food dislikes?_____
_____

3. How does your child get along with other children?_____
_____

4. When you discipline your child, how do you do this?_____
_____

5.   Please give any further information which you believe will be helpful to staff in understanding and caring for your child:_____
_____
_____
_____

RELEASE FORM

PROGRAM DIRECTORY INFORMATION RELEASE

I DO I DO NOT (Circle one) give permission to have the child care program directors and staff print the **full name of my enrolled child, the name(s) of the parent(s) with whom he/she lives, and the family's home address and phone number,** in a directory which will be distributed to all of the families of children enrolled in the program.

_____   _____
Date   Signature of Parent/Guardian/Custodian

RECORDS RELEASE AUTHORIZATION

I hereby authorize and request (name of school)_____to release to the Before & After School Program a copy of the **most recent immunization certificate and physical examination record** of (name of child)_____ present in their school record file.

_____   _____
Date   Signature of Parent/Guardian/Custodian

PICTURE RELEASE

I DO I DO NOT (Circle one) give permission to have my child appear in any **media coverage** approved by the Before and After School Program.

_____   _____
Date   Signature of Parent/Guardian/Custodian

RELEASE FORM

TRAVEL AUTHORIZATION

I DO I DO NOT (Circle one) give permission for my child _____
to leave the Before and After School Program for trips in a car or on public transportation, to special places, walks to the park, shopping trips, etc. I understand that I will be notified before each such activity.

Restrictions on such trips:

Each child riding in an automobile will be secured in a seat belt.

Additional restrictions set by parents:

_____
Date   Signature of Parent/Guardian/Custodian

Parent: This form may be omitted if your child has a physical examination form in his/her school file. Indicate if there is an exam form in your child's school file: _____ Yes. _____ No.

PHYSICAL ASSESSMENT & HEALTH FORM

1. HEALTH STATEMENT - To be completed by parent.

Child's Full Name   **Birth Date**

1. Significant illnesses and surgeries child has had (give age at time):_____

2. Any special health-related needs of child (allergies, medications, injuries, etc.):_____

2. PHYSICAL ASSESSMENT - To be completed by a physician or his/her designee.

1. Is there any condition of vision, hearing or speech of which the child care program should be aware, or could compensate for by appropriate action?_____

2. Is this child subject to any conditions which limit classroom activities or physical education?

3. Is this child subject to any condition which may result in an emergency situation? _____

4. Is this child subject to any mental or physical condition for which he/she should remain under periodic medical observation?_____

5. Are immunizations up to date? ____ Yes. ____ No. If no, what is needed?_____

6. Other significant findings:_____

He/She IS IS NOT (Circle) physically and emotionally able to participate in the Program. Recommendations:_____

Date of Examination_____Doctor's Signature_____
                                                 Address_____

PARENTAL EMERGENCY MEDICAL CONSENT
This form must be presented upon admission for treatment.

Child's Full Name: _____ **Birth Date:** _____

  In the event that my child (listed above) may require medical and/or surgical care while I am out of the city or unable to be reached, I hereby give my consent to medical and/or surgical treatment to _____ hospital and Doctor_____ or his/her designee to provide this care. I agree to pay all the costs and fees contingent on any emergency medical care and/or treatment for my child as secured or authorized under this consent. (The Before & After School Program states that every effort will be made to notify parents/guardians immediately in case of emergency.)

1. Parents/Guardians/Custodians With Whom The Child Resides:

1. Name _____ Relationship to Child _____
  Address _____ Employer _____
  Home Phone _____ Work Phone _____
2. Name _____ Relationship to Child _____
  Address _____ Employer _____
  Home Phone _____ Work Phone _____

2. Persons who are authorized to pick up child if parents are unavailable:

1. Name _____ Relationship to Child _____
  Address _____ Employer _____
  Home Phone _____ Work Phone _____
2. Name _____ Relationship to Child _____
  Address _____ Employer _____
  Home Phone _____ Work Phone _____

3. Custody Restraints/Person(s) Who May NOT Pick Up Child:

1. Name _____ Relationship to Child _____
  Name _____ Relationship to Child _____
  Name _____ Relationship to Child _____

4. Information:

Doctor _____ Phone _____ Address _____
Last Tetanus _____ Allergies _____
Medication _____ Religious Preference (Optional) _____
Insurance Company _____ Policy Holders's I.D. _____

This consent will be in effect beginning (date)_____ and continuing while the child is enrolled in this facility.

_____   _____
Signature Parent/Guardian   Date Signature Parent/Guardian   Date

ARRIVAL/DEPARTURE PROCEDURES FORM

_____(Name of Child) has permission to arrive at and leave the Before & School Program during the scheduled Program hours in which he/she is enrolled according to these arrangements:

BEFORE SCHOOL   Circle days of the week child is enrolled: M T W TH F

Time of Arrival At Program	Person Who Is Responsible for Child Before Arrival
M	
T	
W	
TH	
F	

Time of Departure From Program	Destination	Person Who Is Responsible for Child Upon Departure
M		
T		
W		
TH		
F		

AFTER SCHOOL   Circle days of the week child is enrolled: M T W TH F

Time of Arrival From Program	Person Who Is Responsible for Child Before Arrival
M	
T	
W	
TH	
F	

Time of Departure From Program	Destination	Person Who Is Responsible for Child Upon Departure
M		
T		
W		
TH		
F		

I understand the Before & After School Program accepts responsibility for my child upon his/her arrival at the Program facilities. The Before & After School Program will not be responsible after my child leaves the Program as authorized above. I understand that any changes to these arrangements must be in writing on a Arrival/Departure form.

_____   _____
Date   Signature of Parent/Guardian/Custodian

CHANGE IN ARRIVAL/DEPARTURE PROCEDURES FORM

_____(Full Name of Child) has permission to arrive at and leave the Before & School Program during the scheduled Program hours in which he/she is enrolled according to the following schedule. This schedule will start_____ and terminate_____.

MORNING PROGRAM   Circle days of the week child is enrolled: M T W TH F

Time of Arrival At Program		**Person Who Is Responsible for Child Before Arrival**
M		
T		
W		
TH		
F		

Time of Departure From Program	**Destination**	**Person Who Is Responsible for Child Upon Departure**
M		
T		
W		
TH		
F		

AFTERNOON PROGRAM Circle days of the week child is enrolled: M T W TH F

Time of Arrival At Program		**Person Who Is Responsible for Child Before Arrival**
M		
T		
W		
TH		
F		

Time of Departure From Program	**Destination**	**Person Who Is Responsible for Child Upon Departure**
M		
T		
W		
TH		
F		

I understand the Before & After School Program accepts responsibility for my child upon his/her arrival at the Program facilities. The Before & After School Program will not be responsible for my child after he/she leaves the Program.

_____   _____
Date   Signature of Parent/Guardian/Custodian

EXCEPTION TO ARRIVAL/DEPARTURE PROCEDURES FORM

This form is for one-time exceptions to the procedures authorized in the child's enrollment form.

(Name of Child)_____ has permission

to leave the Before and After School Program on (date) _____

at (time)_____ to go to (destination) _____.

(Name of person accepting responsibility)_____ will be

responsible for my child after he/she leaves the Before & After School Program.

_____

Date   Signature of Parent/Guardian/Custodian

INCIDENT REPORT

This form may be used for any accident, injury, event or behavior of a child which is considered to be of a serious nature and needs to be communicated and recorded.

_____

Name of Child   Age

_____

Date and Time of Incident

Description of the Incident_____
_____
_____
_____
_____

Was the child injured? (Please Circle) Yes. No. If yes, please describe the injury:_____
_____
_____

Treatment Administered:_____
_____

Was a doctor contacted?_____

Was the child's parent called?_____

_____

Date   Caregiver Signature

_____

Date   Parent Signature
                                       (or person authorized to pick up child)

1 copy to parent or authorized person
1 copy to child's file
1 copy to incident file

MEDICATION AUTHORIZATION

Child's Full Name_____

Name of Medication_____

Please give the above medication:

        Amount_____

        Time_____

        Number of Days_____

or

        Number of Doses_____

_____
Date   Parent/Guardian

MEDICATION AUTHORIZATION

Child's Full Name_____

Name of Medication_____

Please give the above medication:

        Amount_____

        Time_____

        Number of Days_____

or

        Number of Doses_____

_____
Date   Parent/Guardian

MEDICATION ADMINISTRATION RECORD

DATE	NAME OF CHILD	MEDICATION	AMOUNT	TIME GIVEN	STAFF INITIAL

CHILD RECORD CHECKLIST
OF

_____

The following information is required to be in each child's file:

_____ An enrollment form including information regarding next-of-kin information including emergency numbers, emergency persons and numbers, health care information.

_____ Forms detailing arrival/departure information.

_____ Parental Emergency Medical Consent form.

_____ A copy of a completed Physical Assessment form.

_____ Release forms for ____ media, ____program directory, ____travel, and ____school records.

_____ Any record of professionally prescribed treatment.

_____ Medication Authorization (as needed).

_____ Medication Administration Record

Located in the immunization records file:

_____ A signed immunization card or copy of the school immunization record.

Optional:
_____ An enrollment agreement form.

This information should be updated as needed. List the date and initials of parent or staff when information is entered:

_____   _____   _____   _____

_____   _____   _____   _____

_____   _____   _____   _____

COMPOSITE CHILD RECORDS

COMPOSITE CHILD'S RECORDS	CHILDREN'S NAMES	Immunization Card	Emergency Phone #	Emergency Consent/Plan	Health Care Name	Address	Phone	Physical	Pick-up Permission	Travel Authorization	Emergency Numbers	Next-of-Kin	Incident Report	Medication Auth.	Med. Admin. Record	Administering Info	Professional Tx

CHILD CARE DIRECTOR APPLICATION
BEFORE & AFTER SCHOOL PROGRAMS
IN THE RIVER CITY PUBLIC SCHOOLS

RETURN COMPLETED FORM TO:

NAME   **BIRTH DATE**

STREET   **CITY**   **STATE**   **ZIP**

PHONE   **SOCIAL SECURITY #**

EDUCATION - Attach a copy of your Teachers Certificate if applicable.

SCHOOL	MAJOR	DATES ATTENDED	DEGREE

WORK HISTORY/CHILD CARE EXPERIENCE

EMPLOYER	DATES	DUTIES

REFERENCES - When you return this application, contact your listed references and ask them to forward a letter of reference to the person listed above. Try to include at least one local reference. Do not omit any of the information requested or your application will be returned to you. All references will be checked.

RELATION TO YOUR WORK	NAME	TITLE	ADDRESS	PHONE

CHILD CARE AIDE APPLICATION
BEFORE & AFTER SCHOOL PROGRAMS
IN THE RIVER CITY PUBLIC SCHOOLS

RETURN COMPLETED FORM TO:

NAME   **BIRTH DATE**

STREET   **CITY**   **STATE**   **ZIP**

PHONE   **SOCIAL SECURITY #**

EDUCATION - Attach a copy of your Teachers Certificate if applicable.

SCHOOL   **MAJOR**   **DATES ATTENDED**   **DEGREE**

WORK HISTORY/CHILD CARE EXPERIENCE

EMPLOYER   **DATES**   **DUTIES**

REFERENCES - When you return this application, contact your listed references and ask them to forward a letter of reference to the person listed above. Try to include at least one local reference. Do not omit any of the information requested or your application will be returned to you. All references will be checked.

RELATION NAME   **TITLE**   **ADDRESS**   **PHONE**
TO YOUR WORK

APPLICANT'S NAME _____

AVAILABILITY

1. Do you have your own transportation, or can you make bus connections to come to work on time? _____
    _____

2. I will be available   all year: _____   or: _____
                          starting: _____   ending: _____

3. Please list phone numbers where you may be reached:

Phone Number   Location   Hours
_____
_____
_____

4. Program Hours are 7:00 - 8:30 AM and 3:00 - 6:00 PM. What times which you are available:

MONDAY   AM_____   PM_____   BOTH_____
TUESDAY   AM_____   PM_____   BOTH_____
WEDNESDAY   AM_____   PM_____   BOTH_____
THURSDAY   AM_____   PM_____   BOTH_____
FRIDAY   AM_____   PM_____   BOTH_____

5. Do you have a current   Red Cross First Aid Certificate _____
                            CPR certificate _____

TREATMENT STATUS
NON-CONVICTION STATEMENT
PHYSICAL EXAMINATION REPORT

The following information items must be completed and submitted before starting work as a caregiver. (This information required by the Iowa Department of Human Services is similar to the information required of all persons who apply for child care work in other states.)

1. TREATMENT STATEMENT: To be completed by applicant.

I, (full name)_____ state that:

_____ I am not currently receiving treatment for alcoholism, drug abuse, child abuse problems.

_____ I am currently receiving treatment for: (Check applicable service)
_____ alcoholism   _____ drug abuse   _____child abuse

If receiving treatment, please explain:_____

_____

_____
DATE   **SIGNATURE**

2. NON-CONVICTION STATEMENT: To be completed by applicant.

I, (Full Name)_____ state that I have never been convicted by any law of any state for lascivious acts with a child, child neglect, or child abuse.

_____
DATE   **SIGNATURE**

3. MEDICAL REPORT: To be completed by a physician.

I have examined (full name)_____ and find this person to be free of any communicable or infectious disease and to be free of any physical or mental condition which would adversely affect the child care program or its beneficiaries.

_____
DATE OF EXAMINATION   PHYSICIAN'S SIGNATURE

_____
                                           PHYSICIAN'S ADDRESS

CHILD CARE DIRECTOR EMPLOYMENT CONTRACT
for

_____

The Board of Directors of the Before and After School Program at Washington Elementary School, River City, Iowa, hereby hires, engages and employs the above-named person to serve in the position of Child Care Director, according to the child care director job description, policies and procedures set forth in the Before and After School Program Staff Handbook. Any additional duties or agreements between the employee and the Board of Directors have been set forth in writing, are signed and dated by both parties, and attached to all copies of this contract.

The term of this agreement shall start _____ and end _____, subject, however, to prior termination as provided in the Staff Handbook.

The employee will pay and the employee will accept the salary of $_____._____ for the Program year, in compensation for the employee's services under this contract. This amount will be paid in biweekly increments by the Treasurer of the Board of Directors on the last Program day of the pay period. Salary payments are subject to legally required withholdings.

This contract contemplates additional hours of work beyond Program hours by the employee in connection with the activities described in the Staff Handbook. The employee is expected to be available for staff, board and parent meetings, professional growth training, and pertinent school events. Compensation for these activities has been taken into consideration in determining the rate of pay.

The employee will be employed on a probationary basis for two months, according to the provisions of the Staff Handbook.

I have read the above agreement and the Staff Handbook, and agree to be employed by the Before and After School Program at Washington Elementary School. I agree to abide by the provisions of this contract and the Staff Handbook to the best of my ability.

_____

Signature of Employee   Date

I have read the above agreement and the Staff Handbook, and agree to abide by the provisions of this contract and the Staff Handbook to the best of my ability.

_____

Signature of President of the Board of Directors, River City BASP   Date

CHILD CARE AIDE EMPLOYMENT CONTRACT
for

_____

The Board of Directors of the Before and After School Program at Washington Elementary School, River City, Iowa, hereby hires, and employs the above-named person to serve in the position of Child Care Aide, according to the child care aide job description and the policies and procedures set forth in the Before and After School Program Staff Handbook. Any additional duties or agreements between the employee and the Board of Directors have been set forth in writing, are signed and dated by both parties, and attached to all copies of this contract.

The term of this agreement shall be a period of _____ months, starting _____ _____and ending _____, subject, however, to prior termination as provided in the Staff Handbook.

The employee will pay and the employee will accept payment for the employee's services under this contract, compensation at the rate of $_____.____ per hour. Salary payments will be paid, biweekly by the Treasurer of the Board of Directors on the last Program day of the pay period. Salary payments are subject to legally required withholdings.

The employee will be present at the Before and After School Program facilities from no later than _____AM until _____AM and _____PM until _____PM on every day that the Program is in session, with the exception of those days when the employee is gone in accordance with the Personal Leave policies contained in the Staff Handbook. The employee is expected to be available for staff meetings and professional growth training. Compensation for these activities has been taken into consideration in determining the rate of pay. The employee will be employed on a probationary basis for two months, according to the provisions of the Staff Handbook.

I have read the above agreement and the Staff Handbook, and agree to be employed by the Before and After School Program at Washington Elementary School. I agree to abide by the provisions of this contract and the Staff Handbook to the best of my ability.

_____

Signature of Employee   **Date**

I have read the above agreement and the Staff Handbook, and agree to abide by the provisions of this contract and the Staff Handbook to the best of my ability.

_____

Signature of President of the Board of Directors, River City BASP   Date

PROFESSIONAL GROWTH RECORD
of

_____

MEETINGS CONFERENCES TRAINING SESSIONS	DATES	CONTENT COVERED	NAME OF TRAINER INSTRUCTOR & SPONSORING AGENCY	CONTRACT HOURS

BEFORE AND AFTER SCHOOL PROGRAM
STAFF FILE CHECKLIST
OF

_____

_____ Employment application which includes birth date, education and previous work history

_____ A statement signed by the staff person that there has been no conviction by any law of any state involving lascivious acts with a child, child neglect, or child abuse

_____ The status of any current treatment of alcoholism, drug abuse, or child abuse

_____ A physical examination report or religious exemption waiver.

        _____ The pre-employment physical should be taken within six months of starting and should be repeated a minimum of every three years.

_____ Professional growth inservice training year

_____ Salary and benefit records

_____ A copy of the Child Day Care Staff Criminal Records check form

_____ A copy of the Public Safety Check Form

_____ A copy of Request for Child Abuse Information

_____ A certification of a minimum of two hours of training relating to the identification and reporting of child abuse.

        _____ Certification of a minimum of two hours of additional training every five years

_____ A valid first aide certificate

_____ A valid CPR certificate

_____ A filled-out Employment Eligibility Verification Form

_____ A filled-out W-4 (federal) and state tax forms

This information should be reviewed annually and updated as needed. Information complete for this year: (year and director's initials).

_____	_____	_____	_____
_____	_____	_____	_____
_____	_____	_____	_____
_____	_____	_____	_____

COMPOSITE STAFF RECORDS

							COMPOSITE STAFF RECORDS STAFF NAMES
							AGE
							EDUCATION
							WORK HISTORY
							PROFESSIONAL GROWTH HOURS
							SALARY BENEFITS
							STATEMENTS: CHILD ABUSE, NEGLECT LASCIVIOUS ACTS
							TREATMENT STATUS
							CRIMINAL RECORDS CHECK
							CHILD ABUSE CHECK
							CHILD ABUSE TRAINING CERTIFICATE & DATE
							FIRST AIDE CERTIF.
							PHYSICAL EXAM
							VERIFICATION OF EMPLOY. ELIGIBILITY
							CPR CERTIFICATE
							COMPLETE

MONTHLY STAFF TIME REPORT

Name:_____ Work Period:_____ to _____

Instructions:
1. Each working day must be accounted for.
2. Place a check mark beside the date if you worked regular program hours.
3. If you worked less than the entire period AM and/or PM, write the arrival and departure time.
4. If no time was worked, place a "O" beside the date.
5. Directors should account for preparation hours beyond program time.

DATE   AM   PM   PREPARATION TIME
_____
_____
_____
_____
_____
_____
_____
_____
_____
_____
_____
_____
_____
_____
_____
_____
_____
_____
_____
_____
_____
_____
_____
_____

Certify that the time reported is true and accurate. (Child Care Director will co-sign aide's forms.)

_____   _____
Employee Signature   Co-Signature

J

BEFORE AND AFTER SCHOOL PROGRAM

SUBSTITUTE CAREGIVER
EMPLOYMENT PROCEDURES AND FORMS

PLAN FOR SUBSTITUTES

The use of qualified substitutes is part of the plan for dealing with staff illness, vacations, emergencies or other causes for absence is essential. A list of qualified, available substitutes can make the difference between a crisis and a smooth running operation.

SUBSTITUTE QUALIFICATIONS

The state child care licensing agency regulates the qualifications of all persons who are counted in the child : staff ratio of a licensed child care center. Persons who may substitute should have the educational and experience qualifications of child care aides. In addition, substitute personnel must have an application on file, a physical examination form, substance abuse and convictions statements, a filled-out Employer's Verification Form, a filled-out W-4, and required state criminal record check forms. The non-government forms are found later in this chapter and in the Form Book chapter.

SUBSTITUTE JOB DESCRIPTION

A clear, focused job description and description of program expectations of caregivers should be available to each person who will substitute in a child care program and to other staff members who will work with the substitute on his or her days of employment.

Some boards mail a copy of the job description and expectations, along with other information in the form of a Substitute Handbook to all persons whose applications are accepted to serve as substitutes. Sample substitute caregiver job descriptions and program expectations are given later in this chapter.

ABSENCE OF THE CHILD CARE DIRECTOR

The following sample job description is very similar to the description for a Child Care Aide. When an aide is on leave, this description is very appropriate. However, in the case of the absence of the Child Care Director, considerations may be different.

Many programs determine that in the temporary absence of the Child Care Director, a designated Child Care Aide will assume the Director's duties for the period. His or her pay will be increased for that time to compensate for the additional duties.

In the case of an extended absence, such as a maternity leave, the Board may wish to temporarily replace the Director with a substitute who is more qualified or experienced than the program aides. A substitute assuming the role of Director will need to have a copy of the Child Care Director job description, and additional information as may be contained in the program board manuals.

SUBSTITUTE RECRUITMENT AND SUB POOL

Depending on the size and needs of child care centers in a community, substitutes may be recruited to serve individual programs or to serve a group of locations. A "sub pool" may be formed among a group of alike centers, such as elementary before and after school programs, or among a mixed group of pre-school and school-age center. In some communities, an agency will play the role of recruiter and personnel office. In other communities, a sub pool recruiter is hired by the participating programs to recruit and screen substitute applicants.

Some persons who apply to serve in a pool may be waiting for permanent child care employment. This is good news for centers who occasionally may need to hire on short notice. The substitute application form later in this chapter provides a space for the applicant to indicate interest in permanent employment. Centers who may be seeking to hire substitutes from the pool on a permanent basis, may request to see the entire application and personnel folder.

The application form which appears later in this chapter is designed so that the second page may be duplicated and sent to all centers who are participating in the pool. All pertinent information needed by the centers is contained on that page.

ADVERTISING FOR SUBSTITUTES

The following sample newspaper and flyer advertisements may be used to recruit applicants:

Newspaper:
Substitute Child Care Aides: Washington Elementary School Before & After School Program. Hours Mon. - Fri. 6:45 AM - 8:30 AM, 2:45 PM - 6:00 PM. Experience & education related to school-age children preferred. E.O.E. $5.00/hour. 351-0050

Flyer:

SUBSTITUTE CHILD CARE STAFF

Substitute child care aides needed for Before & After School Programs located in the Washington Public Schools. Requirements: experience with school-age children required. A background in education, recreation or child-related field preferred. Hours are 6:45 am to 8:30 am, 2:45 pm to 6:00 pm. Salary $5 per hour.

Applications Available: River City School District
                                     1000 River Road, River City, Iowa 52240

For Additional Information: Sam Richard, Coordinator
                                     (319) 555-0500

AN EQUAL OPPORTUNITY EMPLOYER

RETRIEVING PAPERWORK

Recruitment should involve a one-time group meeting at which applicants and representatives from the board and child care staff can meet. This may take the place of individual interviews. At that time, applicants may turn in completed applications and other required paperwork.

Later in this chapter, a form letter appears which refers to applicant eligibility and completion of the necessary paperwork. It may be used by individual programs or by the sub pool recruiter.

A Substitute Staff Record Checklist has been provided later in this chapter to facilitate preparing Substitute personnel files.

SUBSTITUTE HANDBOOK - SUBSTITUTE'S COPY

As mentioned before, it is very helpful to persons who serve as substitutes to receive a handbook detailing information related to the job. It should contain:

Program Information for the Substitute Caregiver

Substitute Caregiver Job Description

Staff Conduct

Program and Playground Rules

Names and Phone Numbers of Child Care Director and One Board Member

Names and Phone Numbers of School Principal and School Secretary

Location of the Facilities Used by the Program

In the case of a sub pool, this additional information should be included:

A Map of Programs Locations

A Directory of Names and Phone Numbers at Each Site

SUBSTITUTE HANDBOOK - DIRECTOR'S COPY

Child Care Directors should have the information given in the Substitute Handbook. Additionally, they should have copies of the filled-out Substitute Information Forms (second page of applications).

SUBSTITUTE FOLDER OR NOTEBOOK

Each child care center should maintain a current folder or notebook which can be located easily by substitutes coming on duty. Contents should include such vital information as:

Children/parents sign-in/sign-out procedures

Daily activity schedule

Program discipline guidelines

Names of the school principal, secretary and custodian

Facility procedures including lock-up, clean-up and out-of-bounds areas

Location of first aid kit, file of emergency forms and phone numbers

Information on children with special needs

Location of student equipment and materials

Snack service procedures

Several easy activity ideas which require little or no preparation

SUBSTITUTE CAREGIVER INFORMATION

The following are the personnel, policies and procedures of the Before and After School Programs operating in the River City Public Schools concerning substitute caregivers.

PROGRAMS
The Before and After School Programs operating in the River City public schools are incorporated, non-profit organizations run by independent parent boards. All programs are state licensed. Each program is run by a child care director with support staff. Morning hours are 7:00 am to 8:30 am. Afternoon hours are 3:00 pm to 6:00 pm.

SUBSTITUTE CAREGIVER AIDES
Substitute caregivers are considered a member of the staff on the day(s) of their service. The substitute assists the child care director when the regular aide must be gone according to the job description given in this handbook.

Goals of the Before and After School Programs for substitute personnel are: 1) the children cared for to be actively involved in developmentally appropriate and enjoyable activities provided within the context of a safe, positive and accepting atmosphere, 2) the director satisfied with the performance of the substitute, and 3) the personal satisfaction of the substitute gained from working successfully in the program.

PAYMENT & PROCEDURES
Program directors will make arrangements with each substitute used concerning payment. Substitutes will receive W-4 forms at each school where an assignment is accepted. Program directors will be responsible for making deductions for Social Security, federal and state taxes as required by law.

REFERENCES
Directors will complete and file a short reference form with the coordinator after each sub assignment has been completed. Substitutes may request in writing a letter of reference from the Before and After School Programs Coordinator.

AVAILABILITY AND ASSIGNMENTS
The Before and After School Program directors will contact substitutes regarding assignments. They will give substitutes as much advance notice as possible. Substitutes may expect to be called the day of or before an assignment or between 5:30-7:00 am on the morning of need.

Being on call and ready to work, sometimes with very little notice, is a responsible undertaking. The willingness of substitute personnel to undertake an assignment is sincerely appreciated.

CAREGIVER AIDE JOB DESCRIPTION

1. Assist the Child Care Director as directed.
2. Supervising play activities as requested by Child Care Director by:
   a. participating with children in group games
   b. enforcing safety rules
   c. intervening when children are likely to injure themselves or each other
   d. remaining with the children at all times
3. Assisting in the preparation and maintenance of Program materials as requested by the Child Care Director.
4. Communicating with the Child Care Director regarding difficult individual child behavior.
5. Assisting the children with self-care activities.
6. Assisting with afternoon snack service.
7. Arriving at the child care site at least 10 minutes before the children arrive (6:50 AM and 2:50 PM.
8. Remain at the child care site until the last child is gone and the child care area has been put in order.
9. Be present in the child care room with the children at all times during program hours except in the case of an emergency.
10. Follow procedures to safeguard the health and safety of the children in the Program, which include but are not limited to hand washing, sanitary measures, playground safety rules, rules regarding the use of supplies and equipment.

STAFF CONDUCT

1. Smoking by caregivers is expressly not permitted anywhere on the school campus. Cigarettes should not be carried where they are visible to children.
2. Alcohol and drug usage by caregivers is not permitted at anytime while on campus, nor is it permissible to have the odor of such drugs on the breath or person.
3. Confidentiality regarding information about children or their families is essential. At no time may a caregiver discuss information about children, parents or other employees.
4. Personal visitors and personal phone calls should not be received during Program hours, except in case of emergency.
5. Personal business needs to be conducted during non-Program hours. Personal business includes, but is not limited to: sitting idly, doing homework, reading newspapers, or any other activity that is not directly related to the supervision of children or the directing of Program activities.
6. Corporal punishment, verbal abuse, punishment which is humiliating or frightening, threats, and derogatory remarks about the child or his/her family are not permitted at any time.

BUILDING AND PLAYGROUND RULES

1.   Use of soft, indoor voices, except in the gym or playground

2.   No climbing on school furniture

3.   No running except where permitted in the gym or playground

4.   Appropriate use of Program supplies and equipment

5.   Food will be confined to areas designated for snack preparation and service

6.   Staff and children must remain at all times within the spaces provided for use by the program

7.   Alert supervision according to correct staff:children ratio at all times

8.   Appropriate use of any building signal for restoring quiet

9.   Children are never allowed to move, touch or ride on a TV/VCR cart

10. Children are never allowed to move, set up or take down movable lunchroom tables

11. The building custodian is to be called in the event of need for sanitary clean up of bodily fluids.

SUBSTITUTE CHILD CARE AIDE APPLICATION
BEFORE & AFTER SCHOOL PROGRAM

RETURN <u>COMPLETED FORM</u> AND FORWARD REFERENCES TO:

NAME _____ **BIRTH DATE** _____

STREET _____ **CITY** _____ **STATE** _____ **ZIP** _____

PHONE _____ **SOCIAL SECURITY #** _____

EDUCATION - Attach a copy of your Teachers Certificate if applicable.

SCHOOL & DEGREE	MAJOR	DATES ATTENDED

WORK HISTORY/CHILD CARE EXPERIENCE

EMPLOYER	DATES	DUTIES

REFERENCES - <u>When you return this application, contact your listed references and ask them to forward a letter of reference to the person listed above.</u> Try to include at least one local reference. Do not omit any of the information requested or your application will be returned to you. All references will be checked.

NAME	TITLE	ADDRESS	PHONE#	RELATION TO YOUR WORK

APPLICANT'S NAME _____

AVAILABILITY

1. Do you have your own transportation, or can you make bus connections to come to work on time?
_____
_____

2. I will be available starting:_____ ending:_____

3. Please list phone numbers where you may be reached:

Phone Number	**Location**	**Hours**

4. The Program is open 7:00 - 8:30 AM and 3:-6:00 PM. What days and times are you available:

MONDAY	AM_____	PM_____	BOTH_____
TUESDAY	AM_____	PM_____	BOTH_____
WEDNESDAY	AM_____	PM_____	BOTH_____
THURSDAY	AM_____	PM_____	BOTH_____
FRIDAY	AM_____	PM_____	BOTH_____

6. Do you have a current Red Cross First Aid Certificate or current CPR certificate?_____
_____

7. Would you consider accepting a permanent caregiver position?_____

REFERENCE REQUEST

Date _____

To: _____
Address _____
City _____
State and Zip _____

Please Return To:

_____ has listed you as a reference in his/her application for a position as a before and after school substitute child care aide. Please fill out and return this form as quickly as possible, so we may process the application.

REFERENCE

Relationship to Applicant:_____

Dates Associated with Applicant: from:_____ to:_____

How would you rate the applicant's effectiveness in a child care setting?
_____Unacceptable _____Fair _____Good _____Excellent

How would you rate the applicant's dependability in a work situation?
_____Unacceptable _____Fair _____Good _____Excellent

Comments:
_____
_____
_____

_____   _____
Date   Signature of Reference Respondent

Dear Applicant:

Your application has been temporarily approved, subject to return and regulatory processing.

Your name will be placed on the list of substitutes who may be called for Before & After School Program (BASP) work **after you have completed and returned to me the attached following forms enclosed:**

1-Employment Eligibility Verification
2-Employee Statements and Physical Examination Form
3-Child Care Criminal Records Check
4-A clear xerox copy of either your Drivers license or Social Security Card

After you have completed these forms, I will send you the **Before & After School Programs Substitute Handbook.** Thank you for your interest in assisting the Before and After School Programs.

Very truly,

Before and After School Program

BEFORE AND AFTER SCHOOL PROGRAM
SUBSTITUTE STAFF RECORD CHECKLIST
of

_____

_____Date Application Received
_____Reference Checks Complete 1)_____ 2)_____ 3)_____
_____Date of Temporary Approval and Form Set sent
_____Date Substitute Handbook sent

Dates of any paperwork return reminders or correspondence:
_____

The following information is required to be in each staff file:

_____   Application which includes birth date, education and previous work history.

_____   A statement signed by the substitute that there has been no conviction by any law
               of any state involving lascivious acts with a child, child neglect, or child abuse.

_____   The status of any current treatment of alcoholism, drug abuse, or child abuse.

_____   A physical examination report or religious exemption waiver.
               _____The pre-employment physical should be taken within six months of
               beginning and should be repeated a minimum of every three years.

_____   A copy of the Child Day Care Staff Criminal Records Check form.

_____   A copy of Department of Public Safety Check form.

_____   A copy of Request for Child Abuse Information form.

_____   A filled-out Employment Eligibility Verification form.

_____   A filled-out W-4

Optional:

_____   A certification of a minimum of 2 hours of training relating to the identification
               and reporting of child abuse.
               _____Certification of 2 hours of additional training every five years.
_____   A copy of a valid first aide certificate.
_____   A copy of a valid CPR certificate.
_____   A copy of teacher's certificate.

SUBSTITUTE REFERENCE

_____

Substitute   Date

_____

Director   School

Substitute worked as: Child Care Director_____   Aide_____

Date(s) Substitute Worked:_____

How would you rate the applicant's effectiveness in a child care setting?
_____Unacceptable _____Fair _____Good _____Excellent

How would you rate the applicant's dependability in a work situation?
_____Unacceptable _____Fair _____Good _____Excellent

Comments:
_____
_____
_____
_____

_____

Date   Signature of Director

K

BEFORE AND AFTER SCHOOL PROGRAM

PLANNING THE DAILY SCHEDULE

PLANNING THE CHILD CARE PROGRAM

Before and After School Programs offer a supportive environment in which school-age children may grow and develop. Key aspects include:

Quality: The BASP is not a babysitting service. It is operated by parents and run by qualified staff who implement a program which helps children to grow and develop.

Accessibility: The BASP is located within the school. Children need not walk or use other transportation to go to off-campus facilities. Inclement weather, busy streets and "strangers" are eliminated as problems.

Affordability: The BASP is a non-profit program. Fees are structured to meet expenses, not produce profit.

Developmentally Appropriate: Activities, facilities, equipment and approaches are suited to meet the needs of the range of developmental stages of school-agers.

Safety: School facilities and playgrounds are constructed with children in mind, and are generally in good condition. Staff meets licensing standards for current First Aid and CPR training.

Exercise: Through the use of school playgrounds and gymnasiums, the BASP may offer children many opportunities for running, climbing, jumping as well as organized games.

Creative Play and Activities: Individual and group opportunities for imaginative play are available on a daily basis. The arts play an important part in the activity schedule.

Multi-age Grouping: The BASP offers children contact with kids of other ages. This promotes helpful interaction between children of different ages and developmental stages.

Attention: Licensed BASPs must adhere strictly to, or improve on the minimum staff:child ratio.

Non-biased Approaches: Caregivers provide equal opportunities for boys and girls to participate in structured and non-structured activities.

Cooperation: A BASP is a "home-away-from-home," where children can learn to work together.

Homework Time: Children need opportunities to relax before resuming their studies. Older children who have evening activities may utilize a "quiet table."

Privacy: Children may play in large or small groups, alone, or with a few friends.

Consistency and Reliability: Children are cared by staff with whom they can develop secure relationships. The school environment is a familiar one.

A WORD ABOUT DAILY ROUTINES

Routine activities, including arrival, departure, snack time, self-care, and maintenance of the facilities, are important for the health, comfort, and safety of children who are cared for in Before and After School Programs. Considering the amount of time children spend daily, on these activities, staff must plan ways to help the children accept, learn from and enjoy these parts of the day.

OPENING

Arrival time, and the first half-hour of the session are sensitive times for children. Children need to be greeted and may determine from this first impression of the program day whether or not their caregivers are glad to see them. In order to be available and attentive to the children as they enter the program, caregivers should have any materials needed during the first half hour prepared prior to arrival time.

SIGN-IN AND ATTENDANCE

After children have put their belongings away in the designated spot, they should sign-in, or participate in some other attendance procedure. Many programs offer a sign-in table, attended by a caregiver who greets children as they arrive. Other programs use seating charts, or velcro "In" charts to check attendance. Within the first fifteen minutes of opening, the Director needs to have an accurate attendance record. Parents depend on the security of knowing that the program knows when their child has arrived.

The Child Care Director (or a designated staff member in case of absence) carries the weight of responsibility for the whereabouts of children who are enrolled for care when the program opens. Prior to the opening of the afternoon session, the Director should record school absences and any collect any messages in his or her school mail box. This information should be recorded on the daily attendance sheet.

The program is liable for children who are absent without explanation, to the extent that they must implement effective emergency practices should this situation occur. Effective procedures include contacting the child's parents and/or emergency persons. These actions are taken to transfer responsibility for the child's absence to another person who will be responsible for further action on the child's behalf. The school office and child's classroom teacher may also be contacted, however, neither one has responsibility for further action.

SNACKS

After unloading, signing in and relaxing for a few minutes, the children will be ready and looking forward to snack time. Children may be involved in many of the phases of snack, including preparation, service and clean-up. Snacks are generally served in a group, although older children may find having a choice of snack time or location desireable.

Requirements for types of snack foods, service and serving sizes are usually found in your state's licensing standards. The library list, which appears in this manual, offers a number of books which are geared to school-age tastes. The Program must offer snacks which include items which represent two of the four food groups and are not highly sweetened. Substitution snacks must be provided for children who have special dietary needs on days when the regular snack is not appropriate.

GROUP TIME

Snack time provides an opportunity the children to come together in an enjoyable group setting, hear about the activities are being offered that day, and plan their day. Children of all ages enjoy choosing their activities. Having choices is important in that it helps them to feel that they have some control over their lives. They will look at the program as a positive experience, not just a place where they "have to go."

PROVIDING FOR OLDER CHILDREN

Upper elementary children appreciate opportunities for program input and choices. These children appreciate recognition of their qualities of capability and responsibility. Directors need to provide for other needs of these children, which includes age-appropriate recreational games and activities and space in which to work and play which is not overrun by younger students.

Programs which care for over thirty children may choose to split their group, assigning separate space and staff to upper and lower units. In this arrangement, children in grades K-3 are assigned to a special staff and specific space which will be most appropriate for their needs. The upper unit is comprised of children in grades 4-6 who will use a separate space as home base. This involves planning a double schedule of activities and scheduling the use of common spaces such as the gym. Staff ratio must be considered in assigning staff to the two units. Among the benefits of split programs is the benefit of retaining the enrollment of older children who might otherwise press their parents to allow them to drop out of a program which may be geared to those younger. Some programs opt to combine their upper and lower units in the morning and separate them for the afternoon session.

Older children may need a time and place for work on class assignments. While programs offer opportunities for children to participate in social and recreational activities, a few children may want or need to work on homework. Many of these students will have a portion of their evening consumed with other activities and lessons, increasing the desirability of starting homework early. Some programs provide a "homework table" for this purpose. Program staff may establish the homework area and guidelines for its use, however, they are not responsible for assisting students with their assignments on a regular basis, or for monitoring homework completion.

ACTIVITIES

School-age Programs should offer structured as well as unstructured experiences to the children. The amount of structure desired will be determined by the philosophy of the Board and Child Care Director, in accordance with the licensing and school rules which guide the program, and the personality of the group of children. Programs may organize part of their schedules around activity centers for supplies, games, and equipment in order that a number of activities may be offered on an ongoing basis. Activity centers offer children choices, while maintaining structure within the physical space used by the program. Centers should be organized in such a way that the children understand where the materials should be used, and later returned.

Center materials may be placed in containers which may be easily transported, such as: baskets, boxes, plastic wash pans, or rolling carts. Some Child Care Directors label containers or tape a picture of the contents onto the container to facilitate clean up, or recognition of items stored on shelves. Many programs rotate a number of popular centers, including materials for:

Arts and Crafts	Clean Junk and Tape
Blocks	Puppets
Wood Working	Science Materials
Dress-Up Clothing	Textile and Fibers
Building Sets	Music Makers
Creative and Dramatic Play	Collage
Library books	Audiotapes
Nature Materials	Murals
Office Materials	Water Play
Food Preparation	Self-Care
Store Items	Plastic Plumbing

Themes may be used by child care directors when planning activities to be offered for a special event or for a period of several days or weeks. Child care directors may wish to use theme ideas from the following list:

Community Helpers Series	Buggy Business (Insects)
Dinosaur Time	Inventors' Olympics
Fly-A-Kite	Indoor Olympics
Outdoor Olympics	Outer Space
Cabin Fever Carnival	Native Americans
Beach Party	Black History
Latino-Americans	BASP Book Awards
BASP to the Future	Circus Time (Clown Carnival)
Celebration of the Arts	Understanding Each Other
The World Series	BASP Checkers Tournament
Valentines Day	Limericks - St. Patricks Day
Halloween	BASP Oscars
Toothpaste Chemistry	Meet the Author, Illustrator

A Program Activity Curriculum Log should be maintained. Brief notes should reflect daily activities provided in addition to ongoing offerings. Successful activities may be recorded for reuse on file box cards or in a divided notebook. While the file may be started by the Child Care Director, it should remain the property of the program. Staff members should be permitted to make personal copies of recorded activities for future use in other positions. The activity curriculum file or notebook will provide a consistent resource, which will help caregivers to engage children in a variety of activities.

Each entry should include information regarding the length of the activity, supplies and equipment needed, and preparation time. Entries can be written on 5 x 8 cards, or on notebook paper inserted into a three-ring binder with topical index tabs. You may wish to include the following categories:

Indoor Games	**Outdoor Games**
Craft Ideas	**Fun Activities**
Quick Games	**Quick Crafts**
Skillstreaming Topics	**Themes**
Activity Centers	**Kid Recipes**

Many activities can be gleaned from the books listed in the References and Resources section in the back of this manual.

DAILY SIGN-IN/SIGN-OUT

Date:_____   **AM**   **PM (Please Circle)**

CHILD'S NAME   TIME IN/SIGNATURE   TIME OUT/SIGNATURE   ABSENCE EXPLAINED

_____

_____

_____

_____

_____

_____

_____

_____

_____

_____

_____

_____

_____

_____

_____

_____

_____

_____

_____

_____

_____

_____

_____

_____

_____

_____

_____

_____

_____

_____

TOYS AND RECREATIONAL EQUIPMENT

The following toys and recreational equipment items have been enjoyed by school age children at various BASP programs.

Sensori-Motor Equipment
Parachute	$92.54
Parachute Record and Manual	20.53

Group Games:
Scrabble	11.95
Double Trouble	11.95
Perfection	16.49
Life	14.95
Risk	19.95
Monopoly	13.95
Clue	14.39
Battle Ship	13.95
Connect Four	12.95

Active Recreation:
Nerf Ping Pong	16.95
Nerf Golf	26.95
Nerf Table Hockey	26.95
Bowling Game	10.95

Cooperative Play:
Wooden Train Set	135.00
Legos in a Bucket	26.89
Lincoln Logs	27.95

Creative Play:
Hot Wheels Car Wash & Service	24.95
Etch-A-Sketch	13.95

Art Materials:
Mr. Sketch Watercolor Markers	5.89
DuraSharp Scissors	4.15

Sporting Equipment
Large Kickballs	5.50
Medium Kickballs	4.50
Intermediate sized basketballs	11.50
Nerf Footballs	5.99

SNACK CALENDAR

MONTH _____

ACTIVITIES AND DRILLS CALENDAR

MONTH_____

REFERENCES AND RESOURCES

The following materials were used as references for the materials in the <u>Before and After School Programs: A Start Up and Administration Manual</u>. **They are recommended as program resources.**

BOOKS:

<u>School-Age Child Care: An Action Manual</u>. Baden, Genser, Levine, Selogson, Wellesly College Center for Research on Women. Auburn House, Mass., 1982.

<u>Child Day Care Centers and Preschools Licensing Standards and Procedures</u>. Iowa Department of Human Services. 1990.

<u>Developing and Administering a Child Care Center</u>. Sciarra, Dorothy and Dorsey, Houghton Mifflin Co., Boston, 1979.

<u>Activities for School-Age Child Care</u>. Blav, Rosalie, et al., Washington, D.C. National Association for the Education of Young Children, 1988.

<u>Helping Churches Mind the Children: A Guide for Child Day Care Programs</u>. Child Advocacy Offices, National Council of Churches. New York, 1984.

<u>When Churches Mind the Children</u>. Lindner, Mattis, Rogers, The High Scope Press, Ypsilanti, MI, 1984.

<u>The New Youth Challenge: A Model for Working with Older Children in School-Age Child Care Programs</u>. Musson, Gibbons, School Age NOTES, Nashville, 1987.

<u>Before and After School Child Care Policies and Procedures Parent and Staff Handbooks</u>. Des Moines Public Schools, Des Moines, Iowa.

<u>4-H Afterschool Program Management Manual</u>. Univ. of California Cooperative Extension.

ARTICLES:

<u>School Age Day Care: Getting it Off the Ground</u>. Neugehauser, Roger, <u>Child Care Information Exchange</u>, April, 1980.

<u>A Performance Based Approach to Staff Evaluation</u>. Johnston, John, <u>Child Care Information Exchange</u>, September 1988.

<u>Financial Reports Every Director Needs</u>. Gordon, Teresa, CPA, <u>Child Care Information Exchange</u>, January 1985.

Step by Step Guide to the Budget Process. Wolf, Thomas, Child Care Information Exchange, March 1984.

Surviving Tight Times or What To Do When The Money Runs Out. Neugebauer, Roger, Child Care Information Exchange, January 1987.

Parent Information Manual: A Vital Link Between Home and School. Hatfield, McCann, Child Care Information Exchange, May 1986.

Parents Need Limits Too - A Challenge for Child Care Staff.   Child Care Information Exchange, November 1985.

BEFORE AND AFTER SCHOOL PROGRAM LIBRARY

Books ordered from School Age Notes - A free resource guide is available from:
P.O. Box 40205
Nashville, Tennesee 37205-0204
(615) 242-8464

School Age NOTES Subscription $14.95

School-Age Ideas and Activities for After School Programs. Hans-Foletta and Cogley.
Kid-tested activities, games and theme ideas. $16.95

Self-Esteem, Volume I. Borba & Borba. $10.95
101 discovery activities to build self-concept.

Self-Esteem, Volume II. Borba & Borba. $10.95
101 discovery activities to build self-concept.

The Table Top Learning Series. Imogene Forte.
Set A: Arts & Crafts. Cookbook. Holidays. $12.95
Set B: Paper Capers. Science Fun. Puppets. $12.95

What To Do With A Squirt Of Glue. Lori Howard. $8.95
Arts & crafts activity center ideas.

Super Snacks. Jean Warren. $4.95
Nutritional snacks which children can help make.

From Kids With Love. Janis Hill. $8.95
Activities kids can do with little supervision.

The Outdoor Games Book. Bob Gregson. $13.95
Group Games and activities. Different!

The Indoor Games Book. Bob Gregson. $13.95
Terrific indoor games and activities.

Mudpies to Magnets. Williams & Rockwell. $12.95
Best science book for after school programs.

Native American Crafts. $8.95
New resource for N.A. activities.

Sticks & Stones and Ice Cream Cones. $9.95
The most frequently child care director-requested book.

Trash Artists. $8.95
Terrific ideas for using and recycling "good garbage"

Gee Whiz! Allison and Katz. $8.95
Fantastic science and art book.

All The Best Contests For Kids. $7.95
Activities related to "for-fun" contests.

The Big Book of Recipes For Fun. $10.95
Lots of practical ideas.

Eat, Think & Be Healthy. Zeller & Jacobson. $8.95
Cookbook which provides activity handouts and writing, art
and music activities related to nutrition for school-agers.

Puddles & Wings & Grapevine Swings. Frank. $16.95
Comprehensive nature activities and crafts.

I Can Make A Rainbow. Frank. $16.95
Comprehensive arts & crafts using ordinary materials.

Kid's America. $13.95
Frequently requested book of unique regional, MCNS activities.
Very highly recommended.

Creative Conflict Resolution. Kreidler. $11.95
Directly addresses conflicts which occur with 5-12 year olds.

<u>Please Don't Sit On The Kids</u>. Cherry. $10.95
Excellent resource for group management and individual guidance.

<u>Day Care Center Management Guide</u>. Cherry. $29.95
A "must" resource.

<u>S.O.S. For Directors</u>. $9.95
Another "must."

<u>Skillstreaming The Elementary School Child</u>. $14.95
Techniques for teaching children to deal with conflict.

<u>School-Age Child Care: An Action Manual</u>. Baden. $16.95
The basic, first "must" for new programs.

<u>The New Youth Challenge</u>. Musson. $12.95
A model for working with 4th-6th graders in BASPs.

<u>Kids Club: A School-Age Program Guide for Directors</u>. Sisson. $12.95
Very practical handbook for directors.

<u>Half A Childhood</u>. Bender. $12.95
Practical information on developmental theory as it relates to BASP programming.

Books ordered from the National Association for the Education of Young Children:
1834 Connecticut Avenue, N.W.
Washington, DC 20009-5786   Phone: 1-800-424-2460

307	Administering Programs for Young Children	$7.00
242	Antibias Curriculum: Tools for Empowering Young Children	$7.00
224	Developmentally Appropriate Practices in Early Childhood Education	$5.00
120	Fundraising for Early Childhood Programs	$3.50
702	The Human Side of Child Care Administration	$12.50
730	Information Kit on Employer Assisted Child Care	$12.00
125	Understanding the Multicultural Experience in Early Childhood Education	$5.50
270	Speaking Out: Early Childhood Advocacy	$6.00

Books ordered from the School-Age Child Care Project:
Wellesley College
Center for Research on Women
Wellesley, Massachusetts 02181

No Time to Waste: An Action Agenda for School-Age Child Care. Seligson and Fink. 1989.

School-Age Child Care: A Legal Manual for Public School Administrators. Wellesley College School Age Child Care Project. 1985.

When School's Out and Nobody's Home. Coolsen, Seligson, Garbarino. 1985.

School-Age Child Care: An Action Manual. Baden, Genser, Levine, Selogson, Wellesly College School-Age Child Care Project.

Wellesley Action Research Papers:

City Initiatives in School-Age Child Care. #1. Gannett. 1989.

Afterschool Arrangements in Middle Childhood: A Review of the Literature.
#2. Miller, Marx. 1990.